# THE SOLO PARTNER

# THE Solo Partner

## Repairing
## Your Relationship
## On Your Own

PHIL DELUCA

Hartley & Marks
PUBLISHERS

Published by
HARTLEY & MARKS PUBLISHERS INC.

P. O. Box 147      3661 West Broadway
Point Roberts, WA      Vancouver, BC
98281      V6R 2B8

ISBN 0-88179-129-6

Designed and typeset by The Typeworks
Set in GALLIARD

Printed in the U.S.A.

# CONTENTS

*Dedicated to Mary.*
*Thank you for caring.*

# PREFACE

Fifteen years ago, when I first began doing marital and relationship counseling, I found it difficult to get both parties to cooperate. One or the other would refuse to attend counseling sessions or would not follow through on the changes he or she had promised to make. And how could I teach a couple to resolve their problems when one partner refused to acknowledge a problem existed—let alone discuss it? I quickly found that in many cases the traditional approaches, such as having the partners express to each other what they thought and be open and honest about their feelings, only seemed to make matters worse. As one person put it, "Whenever we try to discuss something, we always end up screaming at each other!"

At the time, I wondered if this problem could be limited only to the people I was seeing. However, further experience has proved that uncooperative relationship partners are so common as to be the norm, and cooperation is actually the exception! Obviously, if I intended to help couples resolve their problems, I was going to have to develop an approach that would work with an initially uncooperative partner and reduce the level of conflict so that the participants did not end up, as one client put it, "madder than ever" at the end of our sessions.

This book is the result of my new approach, which is based on the pioneer work of Dr. Thomas Fogarty of the Center for Family Learning in Ryebrook, New York, and the late Dr. Murray Bowen from the Family Center at Georgetown University School of Medicine in Washington, D.C. This book is both a simplification and expansion of their ideas. Over the years, and after much trial and error,

I have developed strategies that work even when there is an unco-operative partner who actively undermines all efforts to improve the relationship. Along with these strategies, this book introduces you to techniques that will work where traditional methods, such as "expressing one's feelings" and "communicating with one's part-ner," frequently fail. To help you make use of these approaches, this book will walk you through the obstacles your partner will try to erect as well as the most common mistakes you are likely to make. This is a how-to book in the truest sense of the word.

For many of you, these techniques can lead to a successful reso-lution of problems with an uncooperative partner. However, if you are fortunate enough to have a cooperative partner, this approach will work even better. It works for married or unmarried partners, gay or straight, as well as other types of relationships, such as par-ent-child relationships, friendships, dating relationships, and room-mate relationships. Since these techniques are designed to reduce conflict, limit "power plays" and manipulation, and encourage the development of effective communication, you may even find the in-formation in this book useful for on-the-job situations.

## What is Noncooperation?

Lack of cooperation comes—and hides—in many different forms, some more obvious than others. Surprisingly, whether or not a partner attends counseling is not the primary indicator of whether or not that partner is cooperative. Similarly, a partner's promises to make changes are not true indicators of cooperation. Promises are easy, but changes in behavior are hard. Some stances are clearly un-cooperative. There is the person who refuses to acknowledge that a problem exists, so refuses to seek counseling. How do you resolve a problem that doesn't exist? Then there are situations where people admit a problem does exist, but believe that the problem rests not with them or the marriage, but with their partner—and only with their partner. They may agree to attend counseling, on occasion, but only to help the counselor "fix" their partner.

Sometimes one partner does acknowledge that he or she, or the relationship, has a problem, but still refuses to do anything about it. These people usually blame their partners whenever differences arise, often leading to very intense arguments. Others may acknowledge their responsibility and promise to make changes, but never do so. Still others may act as if the problems were solved and they should be forgiven simply because they have promised to change. Then there are the "saboteurs." Here one partner becomes tired of waiting for the other to cooperate and decides to make changes anyway—for example, to become more involved with friends or to use restraint rather than respond with sarcasm. Unfortunately, however, all these efforts are undermined. For example, when she decides to go out, her partner might criticize her for it, even though he initially encouraged it, or he might change his plans at the last moment so that unless she finds a babysitter she is unable to go. If he also refuses to acknowledge that he is contributing to their problems, she will be back to square one. By this point she is filled with so much self-doubt, resentment, and confusion that she doubts the existence of any solutions at all. If her love for her partner is lost, and she wants and is able to separate, the problem is solved. However, if she still cares for him and does not want to separate, things become very difficult.

Until now there has been no guidance for resolving such situations, because available methods have required, at the very least, initial cooperation from the partner. This is no longer so. *The Solo Partner* offers you a step-by-step guide to resolving relationship problems even if your partner tries to undermine all your efforts. In my experience the popular, widely practiced methods of conflict resolution are of limited benefit to many couples. For example, often when you confront your partner or vent your feelings about a contentious issue, rather than improving the relationship, it makes it worse. As one person in this situation said:

> Whenever I try to discuss issues with him, he sulks for days, then lashes out at me over something inconsequential. Then I attack him back, and we end up more upset with each other than we were before we tried to talk about it.

In response to such experiences, this book offers alternative techniques that do work, with or without your partner's cooperation, where the current methods have failed. Also, they often work quickly—almost immediately in some cases. Some people find they get dramatic relief as soon as they apply what they learned about controlling reactivity in chapter 3. Others continue to apply, in various degrees at various times in their life and relationships, the concepts and techniques discussed in other chapters. In both cases, as negative interaction decreases, positive feelings, caring, and communication return with minimal or no effort.

## How This Approach Differs from Typical Individual Counseling

Many people enter individual counseling for personal problems that are linked to relationship distress. For example, a man has become depressed because of the conflict and unhappiness in his relationships and sees a therapist, asking for help in overcoming his depression. In the course of examining his childhood, his job and career goals, and his present life circumstances, he mentions that he does not get along well with his wife. In individual counseling, the therapist tends to look for earlier causes of such conflicts. Perhaps his mother used to chide him for not eating his vegetables in the same tone his partner now uses to criticize him for some present failure, and this makes him furious. After considerable time and expense, he realizes that his partner's tone infuriates him because of the connection with his mother—but it still infuriates him! An effort is then sometimes made to get the partner into counseling with the intention of getting her to acknowledge, and change, her own contribution to their mutual problem. This process can become very long and drawn out. For many whose marriages are in distress, time is short. The relationship may break up over the next difficulty, or the level of caring may have become too low to tolerate many more confrontations.

As discussed in chapter 1, continued caring is the essential ingredient for resolving relationship problems. All too often, when one partner finally becomes ready to make a change (perhaps after years of being begged, nagged, and threatened), it is too late because the other no longer cares enough to wait for what is finally being promised. It is essential to act before this point is reached, and with interventions that not only work, but work quickly. For this reason, the approach of *The Solo Partner* differs dramatically from that of most other counseling methods. It focuses a good deal on current conflict resolution, offers specific steps for bringing about positive change, and shows ways of dealing with the ramifications and "fall-out" from these important changes. This approach offers resolutions to seemingly hopeless situations, and improvements, along with the return of affection, often come very quickly.

Many years of experience and follow-ups have shown that the effects of successfully applying this approach are long-lasting, leading to continuing growth in each couple's relationship.

## How to Use This Book

You may find that some of the issues raised in specific chapters do not apply to you or that they are minor in your relationship and pose no threat. If so, skip that chapter and move on to one that is more pertinent to your particular circumstances. However, be sure to read the first three chapters, as they provide the foundation for the rest of the book.

If you find you have certain minor problems which do not need attention now but grow to problem proportions later in your relationship, you can go back and use the appropriate chapters at that time, or use such chapters as preventative measures. The chapter on emotional reactivity is a good example: an occasional, minor reactive encounter (argument) is normal and can often be healthy for a relationship. However, when such encounters leave a couple worse off than before, they indicate a problem that needs to be addressed.

Developing a great deal of insight is not necessary for this approach to work. For instance, many people have used the techniques for managing their emotional reactivity to quickly and dramatically decrease or totally eliminate their destructive encounters with their partners. And once they resolved this problem, they felt their relationship had improved so much that they needed to make no further changes. Included in this group were people who had difficulties controlling their powerful tempers. Others had problems with extreme mood swings and the sarcastic barbs they would fling at their partners. Here, too, the simple, quick reduction or elimination of such reactions were all they and their partner felt they needed.

Those who are more analytical or have longer-term goals will seek to apply the methods discussed in this book over a longer period of time. Here, too, analytic insight is not essential for many of these techniques, though it can be helpful. Worksheets are provided so you can apply the material in each chapter (beginning with chapter 3) to your personal situation. Each worksheet follows a similar format. There are exercises to help you identify more clearly what needs changing by both your partner and you. These are followed by working to change what you identified. Other exercises will help you cope with the resistance you are most likely to encounter from within yourself and also perhaps from your partner. How to arrive at ultimate solutions is also included in all the exercises. You may want to photocopy the blank worksheets for further use on difficult problems. Although you will learn much from just reading the book, you will achieve the best results by doing the hard work required by the worksheets. They will help you put the theories into practice in a way that will greatly benefit you and your relationship.

## Abusive Relationships

This book will not be helpful if physical abuse is occurring in your relationship. You must seek protection from the police or a transition house for any immediate threat and then seek professional counseling from a therapist.

In situations of extreme emotional abuse, in addition to reading this book, you should also seek professional help. Emotional abuse includes verbal assault, emotional blackmail, constant criticizing and blaming, character assassination, unreasonable demands, unpredictable responses, and manipulation. These behaviors are not limited to severe emotionally abusive situations. They are present to some degree in many "normal" relationships. The worse the problem, the more these behaviors will occur and with greater severity. Because these behaviors occur in all conflictual relationships, their presence is not the primary issue. All changes that will lead to improvement initially cause an increase in relationship problems. The issue in eliminating the problems is not whether emotional abuse is occurring, but whether you can deal with an increase in emotional abuse before improvement occurs. If you have any doubts, please seek help.

This book assumes that readers can cope with the emotional abuse occurring in their relationship and that they want to, for whatever reasons, stay in the relationship and resolve the problems.

**Note:** The chances of improving your relationship are greatest if you *do not* share this book with your partner until you have worked through all of it. Remember, the work is intended to be done *solo*. Read the entire book carefully before you decide to share it with your partner. If, as commonly happens, your partner will initially try to undermine your efforts to improve your relationship, it is better to keep the information in this book to yourself. However, if your partner's *behavior,* and not only words, indicate that he or she will be cooperative in resolving your relationship problems, then do share this material.

Good luck and best wishes to each and all of you.

CHAPTER I

# The Pain of Change

In life, little of lasting value is free for the asking, and improving a relationship is no exception. Nevertheless, most people still expect the changes they initiate to be immediately and enthusiastically embraced by those close to them. But, instead, change feels awkward and uncomfortable, and often creates anxiety, confusion, fear, and loneliness in those who are touched by it. When we face important life changes we must usually go through periods in which we feel worse before we feel better, since we are creatures of habit who instinctively struggle against change. Unfortunately, this is as true for those actively making changes as for those around them, and there is no way to bypass this obstacle. Thus, though there *are* proven ways to bring about successful change in your relationship, it is wise to be prepared for some initial setbacks.

In a couple relationship, it is also true that when one partner begins to make constructive changes, the two will usually get along worse for a while before things get better. When this occurs, people frequently conclude that the changes are actually creating problems rather than solving them, and so the actively changing partner ceases the endeavor in the interest of avoiding discomfort. The following people's stories illustrate how difficult it can be to bring about change in a relationship.

A woman came to see me who needed help with decreasing her dependence on her husband. In the early years of their marriage, she thought that by allowing him to make all the major decisions she was being a "good wife." As the years passed, she found it became easier simply to give in to his decisions, regardless of how strongly she disagreed with them. Eventually, she gave up her right to decide about even the smallest details and found herself asking him to decide what she should wear, where she should go, and whom she should see.

As this trend progressed, she became increasingly hostile toward her husband. She was angry and frustrated that he controlled their lives so completely. She was furious that he made decisions which affected them in ways that were not to her liking. In addition, she was deeply hurt that her husband continued to become more distant and frequently referred to her as a "clinging vine."

On the verge of desperation (and considering divorce to escape her husband's dictatorial behavior), she resolved to break the downward spiral of their relationship by making some of her own decisions. In the beginning, making this change was difficult. This is how she described her reaction:

> I had a feeling of almost overwhelming panic when I came up against any difficult decision I had to make. I went through alternating periods of confusion, indecision, fear, anger, and blame. The pressure I felt to go back to the old way of letting my husband make decisions for me was terribly strong. It would have been so much easier to do that!

A man who also had decided to change his behavior toward his wife related that when she became upset, she asked him loaded questions which always provoked a fight. No matter how he answered, it was always the wrong answer, and the battle began. After considerable thought and distress, he resolved to avoid these arguments by simply refusing to reply at all. However, this did not really help him because when he did not respond, he felt guilty for not being as "open" as he felt he should be. He became anxious about the possible effect of his behavior on their relationship and fearful of the next such incident.

Another example is a woman who had been a homemaker for sixteen years when she decided to go back to school. The children were grown, her husband was involved in his career, and she felt lonely, useless, and out of touch with the world around her. Even though her desire to become involved and active was intense, and her husband was supportive, she found herself to be her own worst opponent. She said,

> I feel so guilty! I feel like I've abandoned them even though they don't really need me any more. It's always there! I feel it about my children and about my husband. I have to constantly fight with myself to follow through on what I started. I want a change in my life, but my old routine is so much more comfortable!

The comfort of staying with the known was demonstrated by a man who felt browbeaten by his sexually demanding wife. Directly and indirectly, she had let him know she considered him sexually inadequate. He resented the implication that he was expected to perform on command, and instead of being a mutually enjoyable experience, sex had become a drudgery. He decided he was not going to have sex with his wife the next time she initiated it when he was not interested. He described how he felt after this decision:

> I couldn't sleep all night. I was worried that this was the straw that would end our already shaky marriage. I argued with myself all night. One part of me said that my fear was ridiculous, but the other part of me said I was making a big mistake. It would have been easier simply to have had sex with her!

## Recognizing the Obstacles to Change

Once we decide to stop merely thinking about change, blaming others, or making excuses for ourselves, and decide to actually change, there will be a number of obstacles. Just as there is no comfortable way to give up cigarettes or lose weight, there is no comfortable or easy way to change our long-standing behavior. There will *always* be an inner tug-of-war between the part of us that wants to change and the part that does not. This struggle is an ongoing process as long as change is occurring.

If you wish to succeed, you must overcome this inner opposition, and your pro-change part must become the winner. Without this, there will be no significant change or improvement in your relationship. Many people unknowingly set themselves up for failure by believing that as soon as they initiate change they will feel better. Then, when they immediately feel worse, they find themselves facing their first major obstacle to improvement. And that is merely the beginning.

After a couple adjusts to one another early in their relationship, emotional routines and ways of doing things are established that are predictable, though not necessarily comfortable or enjoyable. These routines can include such things as how their money is to be spent, how the children are to be raised, what time dinner is to be eaten, and how, when, and what issues are to be discussed or avoided. In short, each person knows what to expect of the other.

## The Impact of Making Changes

When one partner changes an action, this upsets the established routine for both. If, for example, the wife spends more money, starts or stops going to church, or becomes less involved with the children, her husband's predictable routine is going to be disrupted. He automatically reacts to this change in routine by putting pressure on her to return to her previous behavior. This creates a new obstacle: the partner's resistance.

Here are two comments from women who caused such changes in their family routines:

> My husband has played golf since before we were married. I always encouraged him because he works so hard, and he's inside all day. I tried it a few times, but I just didn't enjoy it. I finally looked for a hobby of my own and decided I wanted to build a fancy dollhouse. Now he says I'm ruining us with the expense of it! In all the years that we have been married, I've never complained about his green fees, golf clubs, lessons, club dues, golf shoes, and all the other ex-

penses. I'm careful about what I buy, I do a lot of housework my-self, and, most important, I enjoy it. I help earn the money so why shouldn't I get to spend some of it on what I want?

When I started going out with my friends after many years of al-ways staying home, my boyfriend began accusing me of not loving him any more, of having an affair, and abandoning my motherly re-sponsibilities. I was only going out one night a week!

Our reaction in such a situation can be very similar to the way some children react when something they want is taken away. Their first reaction is to throw a tantrum to pressure and intimidate the parent into returning the item. During this time, it is futile to try to reason with a child—it only adds fuel to the tantrum. Instead, one waits it out by refusing to participate or give in. The child is simply ignored. Eventually the child will learn that yelling and screaming does not work. When children recognize that tantrums are futile, they stop having tantrums and start looking for other ways to get what they want.

With couples, adult-style "tantrums" may manifest themselves in a number of ways. For example, in anger: "I'm really mad about what you're doing!"; manipulation and intimidation: "If you don't stop this, I'll leave and it will be your fault!"; blaming: "You don't care about me like you used to"; retaliation: "I'll show him, I'll spend more time with my friends That will teach him!"; attacking: "You, you, you! All you think about is yourself!" These are all en-tirely automatic reactive attempts to prevent change. Like the child screaming, "If you don't give it to me, I'm going to hate you for-ever!" they are simply automatic responses to a departure from the comfortably familiar status quo.

The woman who had begun to make her own decisions found that she not only had to deal with her own anxiety but also with her husband's resistance. She described him as being very critical and sarcastic about her decisions. He pointed out every conspicuous and inconspicuous flaw in her decision-making process and was quick to remind her of the times her decisions turned out poorly.

The man who chose not to answer his wife's loaded questions

when she was upset found that she became even more antagonistic toward his new unresponsiveness and began to yell at him and attack him hysterically.

The woman who went back to school had to struggle with her own guilt feelings and also with pressure from her family. Although they gave her lip service support, they complained when she was not immediately available to meet their needs. Her grown children fussed about having to find babysitters for their children when she had to study. They complained that it was inconvenient when she could not drive them to the car repair shop because she was in class, and they said that they felt lost if she was not always available to talk to. They claimed it was because she didn't love them any more.

The man who decided to have some say in the frequency of sex with his wife had to struggle with his anxiety about saying no. He feared that he might really be inadequate, that he was depriving his wife of her conjugal rights, and that she would start an affair. He also had to face a wife who refused to talk to him for three days, and when she finally did, it was in a cold, biting way that lasted for two weeks.

For couples experiencing problems, when any significant change is initiated by one partner, the other will *always* become less cooperative and more angry at first. The result will be a temporary deterioration in the relationship as tensions increase, anger flares up, and arguments ensue. If this oppositional period is handled correctly, the change will eventually bring about improvement in the relationship, and the opposition will die down. Both partners will adapt, and their enjoyment as a couple will gradually return. As one man described it:

> When I changed, not only was I scared and confused but my wife became considerably more belligerent. This lasted a good period of time. But as my own fears disappeared so did her resistance. We've done much better together ever since.

## There Can Be No Pain-Free Solution

Just as there is no way to avoid the inner discomfort of change, there is no way you can bypass this initial period of opposition by your partner. A person has to live through this before the relationship can begin to improve. Indeed, the point of opposition is where significant change will occur. To give up making your change at the first sign of resistance is to lock yourself into a situation that will never improve. This is the challenge you must face when you decide to resolve your relationship problems: there is no pain-free solution. It will hurt no matter what you do, and it is going to get worse before it gets better. If you decide not to upset the status quo, your problems will continue indefinitely. You *can* make changes that will eventually improve your relationship, but both you and your partner will hurt significantly more at first. *There can be no immediate and pain-free road to improvement.*

Since pain is unavoidable, you have just two choices. You can put that pain to constructive use to resolve your relationship problems once and for all, or you can drag the pain out over the rest of the life of your relationship. If you make the latter choice, you will cause all the caring you feel for your partner to eventually drain away. The following contrasting comments bring these alternatives to life. The first one illustrates the choice of keeping to the status quo: "My relationship with my wife is worse than ever. I've hurt for the past twenty-five years and have nothing to show for it." Compare this to: "This past year has been the most painful year of my marriage, but a lot has been accomplished. I get along better with my husband, and the end of our problems appear to be in sight."

Another line of reasoning that prevents successful change was expressed by a woman who said, "I want my marriage to improve, but I don't want anyone in the family to be angry or hurt any more. There is already enough anger and hurt." And though her words express wishes and hopes that everyone harbors, they are unrealistic. Change, by its very nature, causes everyone involved to be hurt and angry. Those who want their troubled relationship to improve, but also expect to avoid any further hurt, will go to their graves waiting for something that will never happen.

You may say, "But how can I change if my partner won't cooperate?" Well, in all my years as a marriage therapist, I have found few things that I can accept as absolute truths, but I *have* found that the most complacent partner will not cooperate—or at least not at first. Your partner will only become cooperative *after* a period of opposing your changes, and you will have to change *in spite of* this. The simple fact is that if neither partner is willing to make changes in the face of opposition, the risk of losing the relationship is extremely high. It is essential that you act while you still care for your mate, because once this caring is gone, it will be too late.

One woman said of this kind of experience:

> My husband was attacking and belligerent toward me for much of our marriage. I did nothing about it and continued to take it. I kept hoping he would see my side of things. I thought that if I explained it enough times, cried enough tears, and yelled loudly enough, he would change. During this time, I grew more and more resentful toward him. It was terrible. Finally he decided that our marriage did need work and he agreed to work on it; but by that time it was too late. I felt nothing for him, and I only wanted out.

For nearly all of us, one of the hardest and most unacceptable rules in life is: The only person you can directly change is yourself. An important second part to this rule is that *by changing yourself, you can indirectly change your partner as well*. It is here that your true strength lies, and this book will demonstrate how to use this to improve your relationship.

Many people consider initiating change a sign of weakness. They think, "If I change first, that indicates that I'm the weak one. If I have to change it's like admitting that I'm wrong." In reality, choosing to change is a sign of strength. It takes considerable courage and fortitude to do what needs to be done to overcome the obstacles that stand in the way of change—and especially to do so without any guarantee of a good outcome. The less courageous often want guarantees that their efforts will pay off; they may give up at the first obstacle, or be unable to acknowledge or correct their own shortcomings. Anyone who takes the first step to significantly improve a relationship is both wise and very courageous.

## Who Will Have to Change?

The belief that change has to be brought about by both parties, expressed as, "My partner has to do his part, too—I can't do it by myself," is only partially correct. In reality, this rarely happens and, indeed, is not even necessary. One person's changes can make a bigger difference for both parties than is generally believed. Closeness can only be achieved by two people working together. But if you are already at odds with your partner, and you are no longer working together, there is little or no closeness anyway. And closeness will not remain as long as your discord continues to grow.

You may think, "Why should I be the one to start it? Why not my partner?" But the question of who is at fault and who needs to change creates another obstacle to an improved relationship. It is expressed in this very typical exchange—distilled from numerous real-life encounters.

> SHE: "You have a problem with your temper. I'd be happy to go to counseling with you if you'd like."
> HE: "I don't have a problem. You do, so you go!"
> SHE: "Me?! You've got the temper. You need to go, not me!"

A large number of couples are so preoccupied with who "needs help" or who is "at fault" that they miss the real issue. While they are trying to decide who has to change, their relationship slowly suffocates. Then, at the point of asphyxiation, the issue of who is at "fault" becomes irrelevant. Consider that though it does, indeed, take two to finish, it only takes one to start.

Because of its nature, and the turmoil it causes to all parties involved, changing one's behavior is an individual, painful, and therefore lonely undertaking. You will need to remember that initially your partner is more likely to attempt to undo your efforts than to join you. If you approach improving your relationship from the position that it "takes two," you have laid down a condition that guarantees failure before you have even begun.

## The Demand for Equality in Relationships

Relationship change is frequently seen as an exercise in equality and mutuality. For example, people say, "We need to change together. I can't do it by myself," or "If it's not mutual, why bother?" But no

two people are exactly alike in anything. Their differences are usually accepted as facts of life, and the necessary adjustments are made
without question. However, when it comes to making changes in
relationships, equality is suddenly demanded, and because this is
rarely feasible, the issue of equality becomes a stumbling block that
many couples never surmount.

In principle, I agree that relationship change "should" involve
equal efforts by both partners. However, in practice I have rarely
found it to occur, especially at the beginning of any effort to resolve problems. Instead, when you wait for this ideal and very rare
condition before making any changes, you are actually deciding to
perpetuate your relationship problems indefinitely. Of the thou-
sands of individuals and couples I have seen, I have found that
fewer than two percent are ready and willing to change at the same
time their partners are. To be sure, mutual change would be easier,
but many couples who espouse equality act otherwise when the
time to make changes arrives. In many such cases, waiting for the
right time for mutual cooperation contributes to the eventual
demise of the relationship.

In any relationship the one who is most uncomfortable is the
one most motivated to change, and because the level of discomfort
between partners is rarely equal, the motivation for creating change
usually lies within one partner—the one on the receiving end of a
negative behavior. For example, in the case of one man's discomfort
over his own jealousy, it emerged that his partner felt even more uncomfortable about it. While he experienced unhappiness and anxiety over the possibility that she might be seeing someone else, she
was faced with the greater stress from his unrelenting questions and
accusations. Likewise, though a wife may feel drained that she has
to nag her husband to help her or do things with her, her husband
will feel more deeply unhappy with all her demands.

Rather than the cooperative, coordinated steps of a waltz, relationship change is more likely to follow the pattern of the singular
and conflicting rhythm of the '70s dance, the "Bump." First, one
person makes changes and begins to improve. Next, his or her partner reaches a point of discomfort and so is ready to reciprocate.

Those who wait for a waltz rather than starting their independent "Bump" will wait for something that, if it ever arrives, tends to arrive too late—when their love has already died. This, unfortunately, happens all too often. Such a situation was described by a prominent attorney in his mid-forties whose wife had refused for years to do anything about the intrusiveness of her family: "All these years, she ignored the problem, so I waited to work on it when she would be willing to do so together. But by the time she was finally ready to do something about it, it was too late: I wanted nothing further to do with her family or with her."

## What You Can Do by Yourself

The vignettes you will find throughout this book are examples of people who initially had uncooperative, if not outrightly sabotaging, partners. In nearly all of these relationships, in spite of a lack of cooperation and, in some cases, their partner's refusal to acknowledge that a problem even existed, significant improvement occurred through the efforts of only *one* partner. In all such cases, those who chose to change found that their lives became both more comfortable and more rewarding.

In one such situation, a wife and I traced the loss of control both she and her husband were experiencing to the devastating emotional *reactivity* in which they were engulfed. (See chapter 3 for a further discussion of reactivity.) Her feeling that their loss of control was getting more severe was accurate, since emotional reactivity tends to be progressive. Unless it is resolved, over time such reactivity will drain every last ounce of life and love out of a relationship. After identifying this couple's problem, we designed a program for her to learn how to stay in control and not become emotionally reactive while in her husband's presence, no matter how intense his provocation. Her efforts allowed them both, for the first time in many years, to be near each other without screaming or sniping at one another or retreating into sulking withdrawal. Her solitary efforts broke the pattern of their negative interactions and laid the groundwork for further positive change.

In another common scenario, a woman felt frustrated and exhausted as a result of receiving little in return from her self-centered and emotionally distant husband. After identifying and exploring the pursuit and distance relationship they shared (see chapter 8 for a discussion of pursuit and distance), she was able to reduce her emotional pursuit. At that point, her exhaustion and resentment ended, and her husband's self-centered aloofness declined.

In another case, a man was struggling with his inability to communicate with his volatile wife. He concentrated his initial efforts on learning how to discuss calmly the issues of fault and responsibility with her in spite of her persistent attempts to blame him for everything. Choosing and timing his words very carefully, he steered through her evasions, defensiveness, attacks, denials, and blame. His efforts eventually resulted in calm discussion, with her acknowledging her share of the responsibility for their problems.

Another man was consumed by the anger he felt toward his partner. However, he eventually realized that repeatedly expressing his anger was counterproductive, only leading to more anger and increasing their mutual discord. Instead of venting his anger, he learned to look at its root—his own unfulfilled expectations. Letting go of some of his expectations set in motion a number of changes in his relationship that eliminated both his anger *and* his partner's problem behavior.

Every one of these people had feelings of discomfort greater than those of their partners, making them more motivated to change. Improvement occurred when they worked on their own contribution to the relationship's problems, moving the problem for *both* of them past the point at which it had been stuck. If both partners are willing to work on their problems as a couple, all the better. If not, one partner has a good deal more power to improve the relationship than is generally believed.

## Why Do I Always Have to Do All the Changing?

In many relationships, one person does indeed do all the changing. Frequently, however, the changes this person makes may not only be wasted but even make the situation worse. For example, if alcoholics switch from hard liquor to beer (as many do), though they have changed, the change is useless because they are still drinking. Partners who move from exploding to sulking (which commonly happens) have also changed, but the effect on their relationship is still negative. One wife described it like this: "He walks around for weeks giving me the cold shoulder. I wish he'd just lose his temper and get it over with like he used to. As bad as that was, his sulking is a lot worse."

Many people waste much of their married lives making sincere changes that, in the final analysis, have no positive effect on their relationships. Often one partner accommodates the other by excessively changing, e.g. giving up too much autonomy over personal goals, values, friends, social activities, and interests, all for the sake of family peace and togetherness. Such efforts are always genuine and Herculean. Nonetheless, they tend to make the relationship worse rather than better. This is why such a person so often thinks, "I always do all the changing and have nothing to show for it." Nothing worthwhile can be achieved until *appropriate* changes are made.

## About Insight, Our Unconscious Needs, and Habits

Insight is a wonderful and valuable commodity. But insight alone is not enough. The world is full of people with insight who are not doing anything constructive with it. The real trick is to apply your insight toward changing your behavior. If a man gains awareness that ignoring his partner is creating problems, that insight is of no practical value until he stops ignoring her. Similarly, if a woman knows that her overspending creates stress in her marriage, her insight is unproductive until she also reduces her overspending. One man described this exact situation in these words: "For years my wife has said she needs to do something about her excessive spending. But she hasn't. Her never-ending spending is still causing arguments and helping to drive us apart."

Some people get sidetracked in their efforts to improve their situation by blaming others instead of changing their own behavior.

Or they may attribute their behavior to unconscious needs that originated when they were young. As one woman said, "I can't do anything about my temper. It's due to my cold father who didn't meet my needs when I was younger. When these needs don't get met, I lose my temper." By doing this, people deny the fact that they can gain a good deal of control over their lives now.

We can develop substantial insight into our behavior, look at our past for explanations of our behavior, or blame our partners for their behavior. However, before our relationships and lives can improve, we are going to have to change our own behavior. Rather than looking at behavior as due to unconscious needs or uncontrollable reactions that originated in the past, I find it more helpful to see it as due to habit sustained through repetition. Once learned, a behavior becomes habitual and seemingly unconscious. Our system grows comfortable behaving in a certain way—even when the behavior is causing us many problems. We are indeed "creatures of habit."

## Maintaining Effort: The Key to Change

The key to making successful change is to maintain effort. If we view a certain behavior as simply a learned habit, then our attempts to "break" our habit, and our inevitable failures, need not be seen as wasted efforts. When we look at these failures as inevitable steps in a learning process, we will be encouraged to keep trying. On the other hand, if we believe our behavior is due to unfulfilled childhood needs and expectations, we will view our failed first attempts as due to something inherently bad or weak about ourselves—like a "need" we cannot overcome—and we will give up. As one such person said, "I can't do anything about my pouting. I've tried and failed. It comes from an unconscious need that I have no control over." But instead of giving up (or blaming others), what we need to do is pick ourselves up and keep trying until we can successfully change. Until then, our problem behaviors will continue, along with their negative effect on our relationships and our life in general. That is the all-important "bottom line," and it is also the approach of this book. Most of our behavior is due to learned habits. Even behaviors that are, in fact, remnants of childhood can be unlearned and new ones substituted in their place.

In succeeding chapters, we will look at what to change as well as how to go about making the necessary changes. Everything that is suggested can be accomplished by one partner—in spite of the other partner's opposition. This opposition will also be addressed, and the strategies for dealing with it will be developed.

CHAPTER 2

# Self-Deception

## Our Inner Enemy

Why is it that when we look at our troubled relationship (in which our behavior clearly plays a big part), we do not just eliminate our negative behavior and get on with living happily ever after? Instead, this source of arguments, anguish, and despair continues. Clearly, something more is involved. And this something is that we will not let ourselves "see" which of our behaviors we need to change, due to the very human phenomenon of self-deception and its seductive false promise of future reward. The familiar axiom "We are our own worst enemy "is widely accepted. But how many of us believe in our hearts that this applies to us and might even apply to us in our relationships? As one wife said, "My husband doesn't realize what effect his behavior is having on us, no matter how many times and ways I tell him. Why can't he see what is so obvious?"

Those with relationship problems do, in all sincerity, omit a great deal of their situation when talking about it to their friends, family, or counselor. Most often, what we leave out is our own contribution to these problems. For instance, if a man talks about the problems his partner's anger causes, he tends to leave out the complications caused by his own anger. If he points out his partner's lack of communication, lack of cooperation, and stubbornness, he is frequently inclined to overlook his own poor communication skills, lack of cooperation, and stubbornness. In the telling, his partner's real struggles in dealing with in-laws, money, or the children tend to be greatly overshadowed by the fact that he himself intensely dislikes and disagrees with her family, the things she wants to buy (in which he is not interested), and his own reluctance to take a decisive stand with the children. He doesn't leave out these things because he is bad or evil, but simply because he is human. And being human, we all without exception are faced with the same ongoing struggle: to be honest with ourselves.

## The Challenge of Self-Honesty

Self-honesty requires that we accept responsibility for our behavior, that we admit to ourselves when we are doing something that we know to be destructive, and that we try to correct it. With our egos as fragile as they are, and change being as painful as it is, it is much easier in the short run to overlook our irresponsible or undesirable behavior than it is to admit it. Thus, self-deception is our perpetual companion from birth to death, ready to seduce us whenever we are off our guard. And once this seduction is successful, it becomes powerful and long lasting. One forty-eight-year-old husband stated it well: "Once I started convincing myself that I could ignore my wife, and she would still love me like she used to, it got increasingly difficult to admit that I was responsible for a lot that was going wrong between us and that I had to change." Such self-lies protect us from realizing how we contribute to our situations. By not recognizing our own contributions, we do not have to deal with the considerable pain that changing them would entail. For this man, it was a lot easier to convince himself that he was not really ignoring his wife, that he was just busy, and she mistakenly interpreted this as his ignoring her. It would be much harder for him to recognize that he had cut her out of his life. With this self-deception, he could feel justifiably hurt when she in turn no longer responded to him.

Lying to oneself is not always a problem in itself. It becomes a problem, however, when we expect to receive the reward we be-

lieve we have earned and are met instead with the painful consequences of our self-deception.

A recently separated thirty-nine-year-old man sits in front of me,
miserable and wanting his wife to come home. Yet he refuses to do
anything about his continuing affairs, his temper, and his selfishness. He denies these things are having any influence on his marital
problems. In all sincerity, he tells me that if his wife would just be
more open and receptive to him, then he would not need to have
affairs. If she would just do what he expects of her, then he would
not get so mad and they would not fight so much.

Having convinced himself that his behavior is based entirely on
his wife's behavior, he is free to continue it, believing that he is an
innocent victim in their relationship. Nonetheless, this denial does
not allow him to escape the consequences of his behavior: the continued lack of closeness with his wife.

A forty-five-year-old woman, unhappy with her family's treatment of her, attended a counseling session along with her husband
and grown children. In that session, she described the loneliness
she felt over the family's avoidance of her in spite of how "nice" she
was to them. In response to their description of her frequent and
scathing criticisms, she replied, "But it's for your own good."
When they then gave examples of her intrusion into their private
affairs, she replied that she was "just trying to help." When they
talked about her manipulative and deceitful treatment of them, she
countered with, "If I don't help you run your life, who will?" She is
free to overlook her own behavior and to believe she is an innocent
"victim" in her situation. However, her desire for togetherness
with her family will not be satisfied until she deals with her biggest
enemy: her failure to recognize and change the things within her
that keep her family distant. Until she does so, she will remain
alone and lonely.

We deceive ourselves by overlooking, rationalizing, and justifying our own behavior—and believing we can escape its consequences. We may also firmly convince ourselves that we are only
protecting ourselves from the unfair and unwarranted criticism of
our partner or family. It may be also that our behavior is not "bad"

as such, so we refuse to admit that it is just not working in this relationship and so needs to be changed. The catch is, regardless of whether or not we choose to deal with reality, reality will inevitably deal with us. The personal costs can be escaped temporarily, but ultimately payment will have to be made in one way or another, more often than not with accumulated "interest." This fact is inescapable.

How is it then that intelligent people, who are quite reasonable and responsible in most other areas of life, allow themselves to be fooled within their relationships? None of us would believe that we could arrive late at work and go home early every day without unpleasant consequences. We would not presume to bitingly criticize our friends' families, their child-raising methods, beliefs, or opinions and expect them to continue being our friends for very long. It would not occur to us that we could berate, degrade, or humiliate a stranger and have that be ignored or overlooked. So how does this come to be accepted behavior in so many intimate relationships?

It can occur in a variety of ways. Perhaps things go well in the relationship for a considerable period of time, and we get lulled into a false sense of security. Or we get distracted and preoccupied with work and other pursuits, start taking our partner for granted, and fall into a routine. And it is here that self-deception may enter our thinking. We remain complacent, instinctively seeking to maintain the status quo by tuning out feedback that says we need to change. Once self-deceit gets a toehold, there won't be any consequences if you continue and its own momentum carries it forward. The longer it continues, the more painful it becomes to own up to our behavior, to swallow our pride, and to acknowledge our own errors. As time passes, more and more effort goes into protecting rather than correcting these behaviors. We become more defensive and listen less to what our partner says about our behavior. Finger-pointing and blaming our partner tends to increase, and we see our relationship problems as being imposed *on* us rather than being caused *by* us. Our self-deception leads us to believe that no matter how irritating, insulting, or infuriating our behavior is, no matter how difficult we make it for ourselves and our partner to get along, we can continue in our behavior and somehow all will eventually be fine.

Of course, this notion defies all logic and rests entirely on the emotion of hope or, more accurately, false hope.

## False Hope

The dictionary defines hope as desire accompanied by the expectation of obtaining what is desired and the belief that it is attainable. It is false, unreasonable, and illogical hope that provides the fuel for the engine of self-deceit, which can increasingly drive and blind us. Since hope is emotional rather than logical, it overrides common sense and good judgment, luring us into believing that events will not turn out as common sense and past experience would indicate.

I asked a wife who had been battered for fifteen years why she didn't do something to stop her husband from beating her. In spite of ample support from her family, who had offered to rent an apartment for her, and the courts, who were willing to incarcerate him if she would press charges, she said, "I kept hoping that this time it would be different. This would be the time he changed and would turn out good. Though he did nothing to give me any reason to think it would happen, I kept hoping and waiting for him to change."

Fantasy, or false hope, allows us to believe that the cause of and the solution to our predicament rests outside us—and in our partner. And this allows us to then give up making any changes after our first few feeble attempts. We continue our behavior with the deluded hope that our reward will come without any change on our part, believing that we are entirely at the mercy of our partner. (This is not to suggest that battering is ever acceptable or appropriate, or that this woman was responsible for her partner's abusive behavior. Her situation is only used to illustrate the incredible power of the false hope that can hold us back from making changes.) This abused wife went on to say,

> One part of me knew that it would not be getting better unless I did something different. Another part kept hoping I wouldn't have to. That I would wake up one day and all my problems would disappear by themselves. Someone would rescue me from him, from myself. I lived on that hope for years.

Seduced by self-deceit and false hope, this woman moved past common sense, reason, and good judgment, and lived in a dream world where anything is possible. This is exactly the same as the false hope of the husband who wants his wife to be more sexually interested and responsive while he continues to emotionally mistreat her. He continues to blame his wife for her distance, pressuring her for sex, believing all the while that he is only asking for what he is entitled to. It is the same as the false hope of the woman who believes that she can continue to snipe at everything her partner says and yet ultimately get him, as if by magic, to share his thoughts and feelings with her. Such false hope also allows a domineering partner to continue to believe that in spite of his controlling, manipulating, intimidating, and brow-beating behavior, his wife will remain loving and close to him. One such man, who found himself in a similar situation, shared his thoughts:

> It never occurred to me that what I needed to do was to stop trying to dominate my wife and then we would get along better. I truly believed that if I could just make her see things my way, we would be happy. I never thought she would actually leave me!

It is possible to live almost indefinitely with the fantasy that we can get something for nothing. As one man saw it in retrospect: "I was so preoccupied with my work, so distant and cold toward my wife throughout our marriage. Now we are strangers to one another. All these years I had hoped we would remain close, though I did nothing that justified that hope."

We can also see how false hope lets us live with our frustrations without learning from them. One woman reflected on her miserable marriage of twenty-six years in this way: "I never realized that I could eliminate so much of the stress in my marriage by changing myself. I always thought that he would have to be the one to change. I kept hoping that I could stay the way I had always been, and things would work out on their own." Such hope is false. It is beyond reason to believe that the consequences of one's behavior can be escaped forever or that the outcome will be positive without having changed one's own contribution to the problem. As another woman said, "Incredible as it seems now, I believed my partner would continue to love me, even though I'd been such a difficult person to live with. All these years, I hoped I could get away with that. Now that he no longer loves me, I see that I've been deceiving myself."

Unaware as we are, weeks turn into months, months turn into years, and we remain oblivious to the things we do that contribute to our unhappy situation. Ultimately though, the consequences do arrive in the form of ever-increasing unhappiness, a deteriorating relationship, and most important, a loss of love in spite of what was promised by our self-deception.

The answer to the question "Why don't we simply change our behavior when it causes serious problems in our marriage?" is that self-deception keeps us from seeing clearly enough. That is why we resist change, no matter how much unhappiness or how many arguments and problems our behavior causes. Before we can or will make any significant changes, we have to see ourselves more clearly. For that to happen, our self-deception has to die. No matter how much anguish, frustration, and misery our behavior is causing, facing up to it seems so much more painful that if there is any way it can be put off another day, hour, or minute, we will put it off. Many people wait and hope for their imagined reward until the death of their relationship, or sometimes the death of their partner or themselves. One woman put it in perspective when she said,

> A part of me knew that my partner wanted to leave me and that, if something happened to me, he wouldn't stick around to take care of me. That was one of those flashes of insight I didn't want to deal with. It felt easier to push it aside and keep hoping that it wasn't true. Then I got sick and he left. I was devastated, but I could have foreseen it.

## The Hard Point of Realization

We tend not to question our self-deception, no matter how many problems it causes, unless we lose all hope that our situation will improve. *Only then* do we remove our emotional blinders and begin to question and reevaluate ourselves. I call this the point of realization. It is when we begin to focus not on our partners but on ourselves and think, "Maybe, just maybe, I too am at fault and need to change."

It seems to be universal that prior to changing, we have to suffer through a period of despair and hopelessness about our present course and recognize that it will not ultimately give us what we want and had hoped for. As long as we remain complacent and hopeful (although not necessarily happy), change will not occur. Only when we reach a low point of confusion, fear, despair, and hopelessness do we become open to changing. At this point we begin making changes and our life and relationship improve. (If you are skeptical about this, look back on your own life. Chances are that your most significant changes were made at the low rather than the high points of your life.)

A man who was recently informed by his wife that she wanted a separation summed up why he had never done anything to improve his steadily and obviously deteriorating marriage: "I believed right up to the end that my marriage would improve all by itself. I had no reason not to hope so, until that hope ended with my wife's request for a separation." Faced with the inevitable, he began to address his own shortcomings; he described what happened at this point:

> I had been feeling depressed and despairing for quite a long while. Slowly it began to dawn on me that the way I had been going about it would never work. At that point, I decided I had to do something different. I had to stop being selfish, stop being difficult to get along with, and stop being unreasonable.

Because our honest self-evaluations usually take place only at points of extreme personal pain, trying to escape from our pain would remove our motivation for self-evaluation and self-change. Unfortunately, there is no way around this. However, the bleakness of our despair and hopelessness can become the fuel for self-honesty and the birth of a more realistic hope.

## Grieving for Lost False Hopes

Liberating ourselves from self-deception involves grieving. This can be similar to the grief we feel when we lose a loved one through death. One woman described it this way: "When I finally realized that the situation in my marriage wasn't the way I'd thought it was, it felt like my best friend had died, and I was suddenly all alone in the world."

The following description of feelings commonly involved in the grieving process can help you through the experience of letting go of self-deception about your relationship.

> DENIAL: First we experience disbelief as we become aware that neither we nor our situation are as we had thought they were. We try to fight off awareness of our situation with thoughts like, "This is not really happening. Surely I am dreaming." Some common physical reactions are loss of appetite (which can result in sudden and substantial weight loss), disturbance of normal sleeping patterns (too much or too little sleep), and chronic fatigue.
>
> ANGER: As with a physical death, when we admit that our situation is not as we believed and hoped it to be, we are profoundly hurt and angry. Our initial anger is directed particularly at our partner, who is still seen as the cause of the problem. However, slowly but surely, our anger comes into focus with thoughts like, "Why was I so stupid? Damn it! How could I have been so gullible? So blind?"
>
> DESPAIR: As we begin to absorb our loss, we feel less anger and more hurt. Our despair is marked by profound unhappiness as we feel the full weight of the loss of our dream. We become plagued with self-doubt ("Is there something wrong with me?"), with loneliness ("I feel so alone"), and with fatigue ("This feels so draining"). We experience a drop in self-confidence ("I don't have anything left to be happy about"), despair ("Will this ever end? Will I survive it?"), and hopelessness ("I have lost all hope that our situation can turn out as I wished").
>
> During this dark, despairing, seemingly hopeless and endless time, we realize that much of what we believed about ourselves and

our situation was wrong. Depression is common. Here is how some people have described this period.

A forty-eight-year-old woman whose marriage steadily deteriorated over the years reflected:

Every once in a while, I look behind my self-deceit. It's like a veil being lifted. When this happens, I see myself clearly for a moment. I see all the things I did wrong, all the lies I told myself, all the excuses I made as to why the situation was not the way I wanted it to be. And worst of all, much of the agony I am now going through could have been prevented if I'd just been honest with myself. It hurts so much when I think of this that I can only do it for a short while.

A woman described her own contribution to the problems she was experiencing with her live-in boyfriend of eight years in this way: "All this time I thought I was fault-free, and I've been wrong. It hurts to even think of it, let alone talk about it to someone."

A man who had been involved in a harrowing relationship with a woman for the past five years slowly realized that something was terribly wrong between them and that it would not get better with time, as he had hoped:

I feel like my soul has been ripped out. I've allowed myself to overlook her lies, affairs, and incredibly spiteful and stubborn ways, with the absurd belief that it really wasn't happening. As long as I could ignore it, I didn't have to do anything different—like face the facts, draw the line, and deal with the possibility of losing her. It was a lot easier to pretend she really wasn't that bad, that it would go away by itself. My own stupidity has gotten me to the point I am now. That's the part that hurts the most.

For years, these people put off looking honestly at themselves and their situations, blindly hoping for a good outcome in spite of the contradictory reality. Finally, they reached the point of realization and stepped past their denial to come to grips with this reality. Though such periods are among the most difficult in a person's life, they are also necessary. The emotional pain people experience leads to a lack of confidence and a hopelessness where formerly there was a complacent, unrealistically hopeful attitude about their situation. In the midst of this uncertainty and these bad feelings, true self-honesty emerges, and positive change is initiated.

As with grief over the loss through death of someone significant, it is crucial to move past this point. Change will be productive only if we seize the opportunity we have been given to evaluate ourselves as clearly and honestly as possible.

ACCEPTANCE: When we have accepted and adjusted to the loss of the dream world we were living in, we emerge with a stronger sense of personal responsibility: we no longer see ourselves as innocent victims, free of all faults and responsibilities. We carve out new and more workable attitudes, convictions, and realities. As one person put it: "I took off my rose-colored glasses. Now I see myself more realistically. I also look at my relationships and see them for what they are, instead of what I wish them to be." Our confusion clears, and the despair and hopelessness dissipate, to be replaced by renewed confidence and realistic hope. In short, we feel alive again and life goes on.

You might react to the suffering I have just described by looking for ways to bypass this painful experience rather than accept it, thinking, "Why go through this if I don't have to? Why not just avoid it?" The desire to escape life's pain is basic to all of us, but unfortunately it is not a matter of whether we wish or do not wish to go through this experience. If a relationship is in serious need of improvement, there is no way to avoid pain, and both partners will have to work on their shortcomings, whether or not they believe themselves to be fault-free. And as discussed in the previous chapter, someone will have to find the courage to initiate these changes. Whoever does so usually has to reach a point where the last glimmer of false hope has been extinguished, when it is clear that what has been done will not work after all, either now or ever. Only then is a person ready for self-examination and long-overdue self-changes.

Because this period is such a frightening and difficult time, we are more likely to weather the storm if we know it to be a normal process—the necessary price we must pay for improvement. I have described it in such detail to provide you with the necessary understanding to help you survive it, as you must, if your own relationship is to improve. This period is actually an opportunity to look deep down, to become honest about your shortcomings, and to correct them.

Many people ask, "What about my partner? What can I say or do to get him/her to see how he/she behaves?" This question creates a big obstacle, one that many people never overcome. We cannot get our partners to "see" their behavior more clearly—at least not directly. However, by seeing through our own self-deceptions and facing any personal shortcomings, we upset the status quo in our relationship. Whenever this occurs, significant change for *both* parties has begun. For you, a change began when you chose to read this book. You had already recognized that some things in your relationship were terribly wrong, and you had probably discovered that crying, begging, yelling, debating, threatening, fighting, or pouting did not work. So let us look carefully at what you *can* do on your own to improve your relationship, yourself, and your life. While you know this will not be easy, you have already demonstrated something extremely important—your desire and intention to make significant changes in your life.

CHAPTER 3

# Emotional Reactivity:

## An Endless Cycle in Troubled Relationships

Seated in front of me was a thirty-five-year-old school teacher who had been married eleven years. She spoke about her marriage in an intelligent, calm, and reasonable manner, and was quite pleasant and cooperative throughout the interview. In complete control of herself, she smiled occasionally and offered some practical solutions. The next day, I saw her husband, a highly successful business-man. His demeanor resembled that of his wife—he was calm, intelligent, and reasonable. He talked about his marital problems, and assured me he would do whatever was necessary to "straighten out" his marriage. After he left, I wondered why this couple could not resolve their problems without professional help. But the next week I saw them together, and they seemed to have become two completely different people. Their composure was gone—along with their reasonableness, cooperativeness, and maturity. Instead they were tense, argumentative, belligerent, unreasonable, and at times loud, aggressive, and out of control. They seemed to breathe fire at each other, and it was hard to believe these were the same two people I had seen before.

Conflict doesn't have to be expressed loudly and vehemently. It can also be quiet and subtle. Another couple, after seeking me out for help with their relationship problems, described it this way:

> In the seven years we've been together, we haven't argued once. When we have disagreements, we give each other the "silent treatment," sulking and pouting, perhaps for weeks. Over the years, we've learned to avoid this by not discussing certain subjects. The problem is there's little we can talk about now because we have to avoid so many topics.

These couples exemplify what happens where there are serious relationship problems. It is called emotional reactivity, and it is the subject of this chapter. The dictionary defines the word *act* as something we do of our own volition. *React* is often defined as acting in opposition to some force or influence. Thus, we act when we are being guided by our own choices. We react when we behave in opposition to our natural behavior or in response to pressure from someone else, such as our partner. For our purposes in this book, the term *action* refers to *self-determined* behavior and *reaction* to *other-determined* behavior.

## Our Old Brain and New Brain Behaviors

Dr. Paul MacLean, author of *The Triune Brain in Evolution: Role in Paleocerebral Functions,* has spent many years studying the human brain through detailed analysis of, and comparison with, the brains of lower life forms—particularly our reptile ancestors. His work identifies three distinct human brain components: reptilian, paleo-mammaliam, and neomammalian.

Our reptilian brain—the "R-complex"—is the human vestige of our reptilian origins. It's the part of the brain we share with reptiles, for example, crocodiles. Our paleomammalian brain is the limbic cortex. It provides us with information from our emotions, which stimulate behaviors for our survival and that of our species. It functions in us very much as it does in other mammals. Together, the R-complex and limbic system are called by MacLean the "old brain," or the "visceral brain." It stimulates purely reflexive and instinctive reactions. Our neomammalian brain is the cerebral cortex; it is most highly developed in *Homo sapiens*. The seat of our abstract thinking, it can evaluate survival issues and devise alternatives. This is the thinking part of our brain, the "new brain," which is superimposed over our "old brain."

When we *act,* we are operating from the thinking cortex, our "new brain," and are basing our actions on a "thoughtful" perspective. When we *react,* we are operating reflexively from the unthinking, emotional, reptilian "old brain," concerned solely with our immediate survival. This has also been called the fight-or-flight response. In this response, the brain takes in all of the external information, together with the emotional response (i.e., the probability of physical or emotional danger), and decides whether to fight or to run away. Our "new" and "old" brains usually maintain a delicate balance, but when we are under stress, this balance is upset. This is when our thinking brain tends to switch off and the unthinking reflex brain tends to switch on.

When the couple described earlier in this chapter were seen individually, they demonstrated new brain behavior—calm, reasonable, and cooperative. When seen together, they reverted to old brain behavior—volatile, irrational, and uncooperative. The difference between when they were apart and when they were together resulted from the loss of control they experienced under stress. This loss of control is what happens to couples experiencing serious problems. Their lives are no longer self-determined but have become other-determined. This "other" that is determining the outcome of their marriage is their old brain reactivity. Such couples are reacting, in contrast to acting, toward one another. As one man put it, "Whenever I try to talk to my wife, suddenly everything I told myself I was going to say differently goes out the window. I end up repeating to her what I have said fifty times before and told myself I would not say again."

Like the knee-jerk reflex when the doctor taps your knee, reactivity is behavior that starts when an emotional trigger inside us is tripped. Once tripped, it sets in motion a sequence of events with undesirable consequences for both partners. When in the midst of a calm discussion one of these triggers is touched, before either partner knows what has happened emotional chaos ensues: charges lead to countercharges, past events are dredged up, one issue leads into the next without resolution, and each go-round is more heated than the last. Both partners say and do things they don't want to. People have described this experience with remarks like, "I can't believe the ugly things I say and do to my husband when I lose control. It's so unlike me." And "I know how the fight will end before it even starts." And "Every time we go through this, our relationship loses."

The end result of reactivity is always turmoil, conflict, and bad feelings between partners. Worse, they repeat this over and over in spite of their desire and significant efforts to stop. Unable to stop their uncontrolled reactions, they slowly suck the love out of their relationship and their lives.

## Emotional Triggers to Reactivity

The entire reactive cycle begins with a stimulus that elicits negative emotions, first within one partner and then between the couple. The stimulus and the reactions can vary a great deal and range from the obvious to the subtle, as illustrated in the following list.

A THOUGHT: "When he's not home on time, I get churned up thinking he may be with some other woman. When he gets home, I'm ready to go at it."

AN ACTION (or lack thereof): "I caught her hiding the bill again. It made me sick." Or "I'm still waiting for him to do what he said he would and seething about it because he still hasn't!"

AN EVENT OUTSIDE THE RELATIONSHIP: "When he comes home from work after a rough day, I know we'll get into a fight that night." Or "Visiting my family is enough to get me looking for an excuse to argue with my partner."

A WORD: "Hearing her girlfriend's name is all it takes to set me off." Or "When he uses the word 'stupid' it's all over with me."

A LOOK: "When he looks at me a certain way, I can't control my anger." Or "Her looks can kill. . . . She doesn't even have to say any-thing—she just gives me that look of hers."

A TONE OF VOICE: "Her talking down to me really ticks me off." Or "When he uses my name in that tone, I feel my hair rise on edge from just knowing what's coming."

AN IMPLICATION: "When she said that, it implied I'd done it on purpose. It's that implication I resent the most."

A MEMORY: "My father talked to me that same way. When my hus-band does it, it reminds me how my father treated me, and I lose it."

JUST BEING NEAR THE PARTNER: "I'm O.K. as long as I'm not around him. When I get near him, something comes over me and I get really angry." Or "It's odd, but just being in the same house with her is enough to make me tense."

AN ATTITUDE: Whenever I see that arrogant attitude, my stomach gets tied in a knot."

AN ISSUE OR SUBJECT: "I smell alcohol on his breath, and it feels like a knife in my chest." Or "If I bring up the subject of my family, she flies off the handle." Or "When I see him talk to our daughter in a certain way, I get furious." Or "We do well until the subject of money comes up." Or "I see a golf course and think of my husband putting it before me, and my head starts aching."

These are just a few of the typical emotional triggers that we carry within ourselves. The possibilities are virtually endless. With the setting off of only one of these triggers, a chain of events begins that heralds much worse to come. It signals the end of our new brain thinking, which is calm, reasonable, cooperative, and in con-trol, and the onset of our unthinking old brain behavior—volatile, unreasonable, uncooperative, and out of control. In this fight-or-flight mode, our heart speeds up, adrenaline flows into our system, blood vessels constrict, and muscles tense for action. The thought-ful self-awareness of our new brain ceases, and our unthinking old brain responds. Someone described this state very well: "After I get irritated beyond a certain point, my mind goes blank and I don't know what I'm doing anymore."

From this point on, we don't fully realize, and sometimes don't even remember, what we said and did. And we end up saying and doing things we would never have believed possible. Things are said or done without rhyme or reason, based solely on immediate emotional impulses and without thought of future consequences. A typical description of this state is: "Once I start reacting, something takes me over and I turn into a different person. At that point I don't care what happens." Not thinking, out of control, and "itching" for a fight, we are now looking only for the emotional satisfaction of a reactive encounter—a conflict of some sort. Here are some descriptions of this very common impulse: "I know how to get to her. I look to push her buttons once I'm started. I say I'm not going to, then I do it anyway." And "I get so worked up, I don't want to turn it off. I savor it. It's almost as if part of me is saying, 'This is bad and you need to stop it right here,' and another part is enjoying it and wanting more."

## Infecting the Partner

Once the trigger has been tripped and the reactive behavior has begun, the next step is to draw the other into the fracas. Without the partner's corresponding reaction, the old brain is denied the fight it seeks. Many times one person's reactivity automatically infects the other. All this can happen silently. It has been described thus: "I can feel myself getting pulled in. Nothing needs to be said. It's as if there is an emotional charge in the air. My palms get sweaty and I can feel it enveloping me, drawing me in." Or it can happen verbally: "As long as we both stay calm, we're all right. But as soon as one gets hot this is active infection. No words need be spoken."

If the other person resists this automatic infection and does not react back as the partner desires, the partner often begins actively baiting the other: "He says such biting things, as if daring and provoking me to fight back." Once this succeeds, the other's reaction provides the satisfaction the partner's old brain is looking for, and the encounter moves to its next phase.

## The Escalation Stage

Once both partners are in an old brain response mode and have become reactively engaged, their exchange will escalate, fueled by the natural contagion of emotional reactivity. As one person described it: "Once I 'bite' and retaliate with something smart, there's no turning back for either of us."

Such escalation, with its reactive overload, becomes a major source of the couple's problems. With the other person drawn in, the reactive encounter quickly builds and gains momentum, taking on a life of its own. Discussion ends and attack begins. Neither one stops to think about or try to change his or her own contribution to what is occurring. Instead, each partner focuses on the other, with accusations about who did what, who is at fault, what the other needs to change or do differently in the future, and what was done wrong in the past. In the blink of an eye, a minor disagreement turns into an argument, which becomes a major conflict. The couple's interaction changes from calm to volatile before either one realizes what is happening or can stop it. Eventually this interaction can engulf everyone in the family. As one husband said, "When my wife and I get into it, the whole family gets drawn in."

When one is reactive, one's goal is not to resolve an issue. Instead one says and does things solely for the satisfaction of the moment: to hurt, defy, spite, attack, defend, patronize, or provoke. The result is a different outcome than either partner wanted or had planned for. Only later, when both have calmed down, do their new brains switch back on. At that point, their rational thinking and self-control return, and often both are totally confused over what occurred. A common remark is, "I don't understand how we can get into a fight so quickly and so often. We end up arguing over the stupidest things."

## The Recovery Phase

The storm has passed—for now—and the recovery begins. However, in contrast to the speed of the encounter, recovery takes a great deal longer with various degrees of damage. One person says, "After one of our fights, we're mad at each other for weeks." But often the recovery is only partial, and another common response is, "After an argument, I don't feel the same toward him. I'll never forget some of what's been said."

By far the greatest damage comes from the lack of recovery. A common experience is expressed in this woman's words: "What used to take us hours to get over now takes us weeks, or months, or never."

## The Repetition and Progression of Emotional Reactivity

Once a topic has become reactive, it also becomes repetitive and predictable. People often say things like, "I know exactly what we'll go round and round about. It's happened so many times, I can predict it. I also know how it'll end before it starts." Such repetition of the same issues with the same negative outcome always does further serious damage to the relationship.

The reactive exchange will also become progressively worse. Emotional triggers become more sensitive, and mutual infection will occur more quickly. People say things like, "It hardly takes anything any more to set one of us off. We argue now about everything, and our arguments are worse than ever."

One couple who had been married for eight years could no longer even be alone in a room with one another due to the high level their reactivity had reached. They described it thus: "We do fine as long as another adult is present. If not, it takes nothing more than simply being around each other, and we're throwing things."

Reactive exchanges need not always be loud. As one partner said, "We never argue or raise our voices with one another. But we constantly snipe at each other with sarcasm, subtle put-downs, and in the accusatory way we put things. Or it's implied in the sharp and cold tone of our voices."

There is also great variation in the frequency of reactive behaviors. They can happen fairly regularly and consistently, whether

daily, weekly, monthly, or very infrequently. As one couple reported: "Once every year or two we really get into it. It's as if we're
saving it up." But, they added, "It's years, or never, before we get
over what was said. It's that bad." What is most damaging about
these encounters is not their form, volume, or frequency, but their
repetition without any resolution. Because of this, the impact on
both partners is always substantial.

## The Effect of Emotional Reactivity on Your Relationship

While we are behaving reactively, effective communication is prevented and true listening ceases as each partner talks over, for, or at
the other. One unresolved issue follows another, and each partner
obstinately refuses to change position. Each may dredge up the
past, engage in name-calling or screaming, or avoid responding in
fear of the other's reaction. The resulting tension makes discussion
of critical issues highly stressful if not impossible.

Most couples either continue their vicious arguments over time
or treat contentious issues as if they don't exist. But those who
avoid issues may instead quietly take "pot-shots" at one another.
One such partner said, "On the surface, we appear very calm and
friendly to each other, never raising our voices or arguing. But that
friendliness is really coldness." She and her partner sat quite com-
posed in front of me, but their muted reactivity was glaringly clear
despite their impassive exteriors.

Volatile reactivity makes problem-solving very difficult or impossible. One partner says, "Whenever we need to resolve a problem, after we 'talk' together, it's even worse. The original problem is
still there, and now we're both mad at each other on top of it all."
Another says, "We've got so many problems in our marriage, but
we can't even talk to each other to try to work any of them out.
That's the worst part."

But the most important and far-reaching effect of emotional reactivity is the one it has on the quality of the relationship. It inexorably sucks out all caring, joy, love, and friendship. This is clearly

expressed in what people say about their relationships: "We only talk to each other when we absolutely have to." Or "Our sex life has gone downhill as the hassles in our relationship have increased." Or "We don't enjoy each other's company like we once did." Or "I can't forget all those ugly things that have been said in the past. Every time one was said, a little of my love for her vanished." Or "I love her, but I am afraid to get close to her and get hurt again."

## The Impact of Emotional Reactivity on You

Besides its effect on the relationship, reactivity also has high personal impact. Stressful exchanges leave both partners tense, confused, emotionally and physically drained, and in fear of their reoccurrence. Below are some descriptions of reactivity's personal costs.

FEELINGS OF REGRET: "Every time I get into it with my husband over sex, I end up saying things I can't take back. Then I have to expend an enormous amount of effort to undo the damage, only to start the whole thing all over again. I kick myself every time for saying those things to begin with."

FEELING UPSET AND HELPLESS: "It leaves me so churned up, I can't sleep or eat for days." Or "I'm so upset, the rest of my week is ruined." Or "My feelings get hurt a lot more easily. I never used to be this way." Or "I never used to cry when I was upset. Now I do it all the time." Or "Now I get hysterical over such little things."

BECOMING PREOCCUPIED: "After one of our fights, I can't get my mind off it." Or "After our disagreement, I noticed my body was driving the car, but my mind was somewhere else."

BECOMING CONFUSED: "I don't know what I want. I get so mad I want him out of my life. When I calm down, I want him to stay . . . until our next argument." Or, "After he left, I got in my car and followed him around. I was so worked up I didn't realize what I was doing."

LOSING CONTROL: "I get so upset, I consider doing something drastic." Or "I say ugly things that I don't really believe, but I can't stop myself from saying them."

BECOMING FEARFUL: "I'm so afraid that something really bad is going to happen during one of our exchanges." Or "That wasn't me. I had no control over myself. It scared the hell out of me."

FEELINGS OF SHAME AND EMBARRASSMENT: "I'm embarrassed to be seen in public after such an argument. It's written all over me. I know people can tell." Or "I'm ashamed to see my neighbors after one of our screaming matches."

FEELINGS OF ANGER AND HATRED: "These arguments leave me feeling tremendously hostile and resentful." Or "I get so angry I think I am going to have a stroke." Or "I'm developing such a hatred of him because of our fighting." Or "I'm coming to feel out-and-out hatred toward the woman. Sometimes I even wish she was dead."

FEELINGS OF FRUSTRATION: "It's so frustrating to go over and over the same thing and accomplish nothing." Or "Our arguments over the children have been a source of frustration between us for years."

FEELING TENSE: "I'm always tense because I'm afraid the subject will come up again. I spend a lot of energy directing conversation away from that subject." Or "It's so tense when we're together, you can feel it in the air."

FEELING UNHAPPY: "This is draining the life out of me. I'm so unhappy, I've forgotten what it's like to laugh." Or "I'm happiest when she's not around."

EXPERIENCING LOWERED SELF-ESTEEM: "I'm at the point where I wish I was dead. That is a horrible thought, but that's how far I've come. At least then I wouldn't have to put up with all this bickering." Or "I'm so apologetic afterward, I find myself disgusting."

EXPERIENCING PHYSICAL SIDE-EFFECTS: "I cry and worry so much, it's affecting my health." Or "I'm completely worn out from our continuing conflicts." Or "I'm a nervous wreck because of all the turmoil. I'm taking pills for my blood pressure and headaches, and to help me sleep at night."

BECOMING DRAWN TO DISTRACTIONS: "After we fight, I go out and spend a lot of money. It helps at the time to forget the hurt, but it has added money problems on top of the rest of our problems." Or "I spend weekends at work to keep from coming home to the tension."

# The Benefits of Restraining Our Old Brain Reactivity

Emotional reactivity is progressive. If not controlled, it gets worse, and both partners suffer increasingly. Fortunately, our emotional reactivity is manageable, because engagement is needed to fuel it, and nonengagement will starve it. Although the participation of both partners escalates reactivity until it is out of control, it takes only one partner to prevent it from reaching an infectious level. And here is where *your* power to improve your relationship lies. By not allowing yourself to engage in a reactive exchange—in spite of your partner's efforts to draw you in—you short-circuit the emotional reactivity and eliminate the argument that inevitably follows. And you can do this whether you're on the initiating or receiving end of an exchange. Even better, just as reactivity is contagious, so also is nonreactivity. When you learn to restrain your own reactivity, you help your partner control his. One woman describes this process: "My partner and I went through a good deal of stress as I struggled to stay calm despite all the tension between us. Finally he calmed down, and now he doesn't react even when I'm upset." Because this effect is progressive both you and your partner will benefit when you take the initiative. A man summed this up: "The last eighteen years were terrible, but I'm now getting along much better with my wife. We're discussing and sharing things we haven't in a long time. In addition, the hostility and hatred I felt toward her before are disappearing."

There can be no effective communication in any relationship while there is a high level of emotional reactivity. In couple relationships, the problems are not primarily communication problems, as is commonly believed. The underlying difficulty is the inability of either partner to behave nonreactively, which then produces communication problems. High emotional reactivity will shut down communication, and low reactivity will open it up. Someone described this very clearly: "As long as I'm calm, I can discuss anything. When I'm upset, my communication goes haywire."

By managing your own reactivity, you not only improve the emotional climate in your relationship but you also restore good communication between yourself and your partner. The same holds true for problem-solving within your relationship. Your old brain's function is to resolve life-threatening issues immediately with fight-or-flight reactions, but long-term problem-solving is only possible with your more evolved new brain. A couple must move past their emotional reactivity in order to begin to resolve their problems.

## Moving Away from Emotional Reactivity

To change a reactive situation, your first step is to identify what you can do differently in order to lower your own reactive responses. The next task is to become as calm and nonreactive as possible, both outwardly *and* inwardly, in spite of all your partner's provocation, pressure, and engagement tactics. It's this *non*engagement through self-restraint that will defeat reactive encounters. If you were to express everything you feel, it would only make the reactivity worse. But our reactions are difficult to control not because they are expressions of unconscious needs, which are doomed to be forever repeated, but because they have become deeply ingrained habits.

Changing these habits requires a very specific and well-thought-out plan, which involves identifying and then practicing your new behavior until your old one can be dropped and the new one firmly established. This can be done best over time and in a series of piecemeal steps. *Anyone* can do it. Achieving this is not complicated, but it will require considerable effort and practice. To end your mutual reactivity, you will need to tell yourself, "I'll stop my part, regardless of who started it, who is at fault, and whether or not my partner is also doing anything about it."

You can begin the work on your own relationship by using the worksheets at the end of this chapter, but first read the following pages which explain the steps you will need to follow.

### Identifying Mutually Reactive Areas

In observing your reactive exchanges, you will note your partner's as well as your own. The more clearly you can identify your partner's reactivity, the better you will be able to stop reacting to that old brain behavior. Reactive exchanges happen exactly as described earlier. The more clearly you can "see" the sequence of events as they happen in your own life, rather than as events described in a book, the more readily you will arrive at your own solutions.

Begin by picking a recent reactive exchange (or wait until another one happens)—a tension-filled discussion, an argument, or a fight—and try to identify the stages outlined earlier. In the beginning, it is usually easier to observe reactive exchanges in someone else's relationship. Afterward, it will become easier to look at your own relationship. But once you start looking for it, you will find that reactivity is not difficult to spot.

## Identifying Your Own Emotional Triggers

You will watch for the physiological changes that always occur when you enter a reactive state, especially the earliest subtle signs, as opposed to such obvious ones as screaming. These might include your stomach knotting up, your head throbbing, or your heart beating faster. A number of typical emotional triggers were described above. In the worksheets, you will be guided to discovering what seems to set you and your partner off.

After you've looked within your relationship, note the contribution of outside events. Some typical observations are: "On the anniversary of my mother's death, I notice my husband and I always have a fight." Or "After he comes back from visiting his sister, he and I always get into it." Sometimes there is a time delay and a reactive encounter is triggered by events that happened a week or two (or more) earlier. One man observed, "My wife and I got into a big fight over the car yesterday. But for me what started it was when she called me a spendthrift last week." For many people, emotional triggers recur at particular times of the year, such as at Christmas or on vacations.

You will be able to use your reactive exchanges as learning experiences, albeit painful ones. After you've seethed, blamed, or cursed your partner and are calmer you can look back on the actual events and trace them out. They are trying to tell you something, so listen to them! In the worksheets, when you start to ask yourself such questions as, "Was it something I said or she said?" look at yourself to observe your own anxiety and resistance. You may notice that these questions make you feel very tense. Try to get past this point by confronting it, and asking yourself as many uncomfortable questions as you can handle. Remember the long-term consequences of self-deception, and don't let yourself be seduced any longer by its false promises. No one is an innocent victim in emotionally reactive exchanges, and both partners share equal responsibility for them. Until you discover your own contributions to the reactive exchanges in your relationship, you will continue to suffer their destructive consequences.

### Reactive Infection and Escalation in Your Relationship

There are many things your partner may do after an emotional trigger is pulled. Some common reactions are screaming, sulking, criticizing, spending money, taking things out on the children, becoming depressed, becoming withdrawn. You may then react in many ways. You may, for example, discover a pattern of provocation and baiting between you and your partner. I am often asked such questions as, "Am I just imagining it or is my partner really trying to provoke me?" Often the answer is yes, there is more provocation in troubled relationships than people generally realize. Another frequent question is, "Why is my husband doing this? Why would he want to bait me into a fight?" The answer is that this is a fight-or-flight old brain response. Once activated, it will try for a fight, even if it has to intentionally provoke one. A common further question is, "If my girlfriend is baiting me, does that mean I am also baiting her?" Again, the answer is often yes. Most people believe they are not provoking their partners. They may not realize when they do so, but because they are human, they *are* doing so—particularly at times of great stress. But when they drop their provocation, a significant part of their relationship's reactivity is eliminated.

Occasionally people will report, "Sometimes nothing happens to trigger it! We're getting along fine, and then one of us picks a fight for no apparent reason." This happens because reactive habits die hard, and people become emotionally accustomed to them. When this is the situation, a period of calm can actually create discomfort in both partners, which then becomes a signal for the old brain to initiate a fight. This is why some people will say, "Things cannot be calm between us for too long before one of us provokes an argument."

Understanding this pattern will help you identify how reactive infection is taking place between you and your partner. You may even learn to see the infection happening on a nonverbal level. Some people can even sense it in the air. As one man said, "I can feel it when I get in the same room with her. I don't even have to see her."

You may notice the beginning of the reactive infection by observing the nature of your partner's provocation. It may be loud and obvious, as one woman described: "He screams at me until I finally scream back." Or it may be more subtle: "She knows the subjects that bother me, but she manages to drop them in the conversation anyway." It may also be indirect. One husband described such a situation: "She introduces a subject to a neighbor or her family when I'm within hearing that's a put-down of something I have done. That she knows I hear it bothers me."

As you use the worksheets, you may discover that you do bait your mate by using a provocative word or introducing a sensitive issue, by a change in your tone of voice or by not doing something. You can discover how you yourself start a reactive exchange by watching your partner's reactions to what you say and then tracing those reactions to their source. You will soon learn to keep an eye turned toward what is first said and done by each of you to disturb the peace, when things are calm between you. Once you and your partner have become reactively engaged, you will learn to observe what follows, and you may discover a certain point that signals the loss of control, when it becomes impossible for you to stop your reaction. This moment is when escalation begins. Being able to identify this moment will be of use to you later on.

You will need to sensitize yourself to the effects of reactivity because we often become numbed by them, tending to overlook and dismiss them. However, if you look closely enough, you will see that reactivity is exacting a higher cost on your life and relationship than you have realized. Many times, reactive exchanges take place so quickly and subtly, that all you can see are the telltale aftereffects. As one woman described it: "I can't put my finger on what happened between us. All I know is I ended up confused and upset." If you start paying attention to such signals in your own life, you can use them to help you discover their source.

### Obstacles to Communication and Problem-Solving in Your Relationship

With the help of the worksheets at the end of this chapter, you can learn to recognize the changes in your mutual communication by comparing the differences between when you both are calm and when you become reactive. You will note how each cuts the other off, how you use certain words, how the volume and tone of your voices change, at what point listening tends to stop and the subject under discussion switches, as well as which subjects are most often changed. You can make the same observations for problem-solving. After a reactive exchange with your partner, you will discover how little was accomplished and see the high cost of unresolved issues.

You will also be able to discover if there is an element of timing in your reactive encounters. Because reactivity is repetitive, consistent, and predictable, you can turn this predictability to your advantage by studying the situation and yourself until you see a pattern emerging.

As you can see, this approach is not geared toward a "quick fix." It takes a good deal of effort over a significant period of time. However, you will have plenty of time to undo reactivity's insidious effects because, unfortunately, they will be ongoing until something constructive can be done.

## Managing Your Own Reactivity

As it's always easier to prevent a reactive interaction from starting than it is to stop one after it's begun, you will need to learn how to communicate in potentially reactive situations. When you have observed at least one of your own behaviors precipitating a reactive encounter, you will be able to focus your efforts on managing it differently. Once you have been successful with one, you can go on to another. While eliminating one behavior may or may not have a great overall effect on your relationship, the more such behaviors you eliminate, the more powerful the impact will be. The following comments by various people describe how they first began to identify their own reactive behavior.

> I've observed that when I'm worked up, it's a bad time for me to discuss issues. I end up lecturing her.

> When my husband is disciplining the children and I get between them, it leads to an argument.

> When she makes a mistake and I say 'I told you so,' it's followed by significant tension between us.

Before you can alter your reactivity, you will need to remember and picture your old behavior, slowing it down, frame by frame, leaving out as few details as possible. Then, the next time, you may be able to keep yourself from saying something reactive. If this is too difficult to do while you are with your partner, you may have to use physical distance or involvement with something else to help calm yourself down, and keep you from infecting your mate. Since reactive infection can happen by simply being in close proximity to your partner, use distance to keep it from developing. This is especially helpful if the agitated partner can then return in a calmer state. Go to a different room for a while, go for a walk, call a friend to talk about it, write about it in a journal, or immerse yourself in a book or hobby. You might need to do all of these things at different times.

You may believe that leaving a confrontation is an expression of defeat, like running away from an issue. But in our relationships, there are times to run and times to confront, and sometimes "flight" is more appropriate than "fight." Just before an imminent reactive exchange is the time to run, because the only thing you can accomplish by staying to deal with the issue is to make it worse. Rather than continuing to say and do things you both will regret for a long time, it's better to leave the situation. Thus, a good rule of thumb is that when you feel the exchange getting out of control—withdraw. Only when you are both calmer and back in control can the issue be dealt with by discussing it.

Also, recognize that there is no graceful way to retreat. Most partners will initially perceive it as sulking or retaliation (which in many cases it has been). Whatever the initial perceptions and motives, the value of breaking off is to give both partners time to get back into their new brain. You will have to struggle to overcome any injured pride reactions, and to not needlessly prolong your detachment by, for instance, sulking. Further, if you find yourself harboring such feelings, you disengaged too late and the infection already occurred.

Likewise, there are appropriate times to reveal what you are feeling to your partner, and times when it is wise not to. Only after you've calmed down and are back in control is it possible to express your feelings to your partner without triggering a reactive exchange. Before that point, you will be reacting with your old brain, which will be looking for a confrontation rather than a resolution. It is essential to find ways to avoid reactivity that work for you and then incorporate them into your ongoing behavior. The ideas discussed below include suggestions for you to consider, though you will find others to suit you as well.

If it is a look that often triggers your loss of control, you could plan a way of avoiding that look. If it's the smell of alcohol, you might keep your distance after your partner comes home from a night with his friends, or you might choose to do something different once you notice the smell of alcohol. At this point, you will be struggling largely with yourself—strengthening your new brain response by retraining it to override your old brain. Like an unused muscle, the new brain either atrophies or grows stronger depending on how much it is used. A later chapter discusses what you can do if perpetual disengagement is a problem in your relationship, if, as one woman put it, "He won't argue or engage with me in anything!"

## Dealing With Your Inner Opposition
You will find that as you work through the worksheets at the end of this chapter, your biggest struggle will be with yourself, between

giving up or continuing your old behavior. A part of you will want to continue it, and a part of you will want to stop it. You will feel fear, confusion, indecision, self-doubt, and despair. You will also feel anger at your partner. Such anger is a valuable emotion that can be turned into a powerful motivator and used productively to your own advantage instead of simply being vented on your partner. (For a comprehensive discussion of anger, see chapter 7.) Because you have probably been repeating this pattern for many years, un-learning it will feel unnatural and awkward for a while, as doing anything new often feels. However, with repetition, it will become much more natural and easier for you. Since you are dealing with an emotional habit, be prepared to fail in your first attempts. At this early stage, many people assume that either they, or this approach, are hopeless—and give up. But remember that you are dealing with a long-established habit that will take time and a good deal of repe-tition to change.

## The Process of Changing Reactive Behavior

I have observed four distinct stages everyone goes through as he or she begins to work on changing a behavior. These are described be-low, together with very typical comments from a woman who struggled to change her behavior.

In the first stage, what needs changing is identified, and an alter-native behavior is planned: "The next time I'm upset, instead of im-mediately confronting him, I'm going to go for a walk until I'm calmer." In the next stage, when a difficult situation comes up, her mind seems to go blank (as the old brain automatically takes over once again), and she behaves as usual. Later, when she's calmer, she remembers what she had planned to carry out: "I got upset and I jumped on him like I always do. I completely forgot what I was go-ing to do differently until after it was over."

In the third stage, though she recognized the situation when it arose again, she was still unable to change her behavior: "He came home and I jumped on him—as usual. But this time I was aware of what I was doing—I just couldn't stop myself."

In the last stage, she followed through with her new behavior and reported: "He came home, I saw what was about to happen, and I was able to go for a walk until I was calmer, rather than confronting him."

Few people can skip any of these stages, though they pass through them at varying speeds. Some pass through them quickly, but the majority stay in each one for quite a while before moving on to the next. Each time you fail, you can learn something by focusing on the mistakes you, rather than your partner, made. If, in an interaction, you find yourself feeling confused, this is a sign of reactive overload. When this happens, back out, cool off, and only re-enter it once you have your exact behavior preplanned. Using the worksheets, prepare yourself with suitable ways to end it when you have already started to become reactive, and then try again after you're calmer. With every failure, you will become stronger, more insightful, and closer to eliminating your problems.

Be careful not to get sidetracked by focusing on the past with such questions as, "Why is this happening? How has it come about that I and my partner behave this way?" Just keep clearly in mind that until you change that behavior, it will continue its drain on your life and relationship. There can be no exceptions to this rule. You will need to ride out your initial, temporary discomfort, seeing it for what it is—a sign of impending success rather than of failure. You can use the four stages of change as a yardstick to measure how close you are to successfully changing, and remember it can take months between identifying what needs to be changed and successfully changing it. Each time you change one reactive behavior, you can move on to another. You will find that the first few changes are the most awkward and difficult, after which it will become easier (though never easy). The more such changes you make, the more their impact will accumulate.

In spite of all your efforts, do not expect your relationship to improve immediately because your partner will be trying to escalate the reactivity between you to restore the known, mutually familiar pattern of interactions. For this reason, it is best to keep your plan and goal to yourself. *Do not disclose it to your partner before his or her opposition has fully passed and your situation has substantially improved.*

That you may provoke your partner into leaving you must be considered as a real possibility. But if you wish the relationship to improve, it is a risk that cannot be avoided. If you do not take it, the relationship will continue to deteriorate. If you are unable to act because of your great fear of losing your partner, perhaps seeking the help of a therapist or counselor (for yourself alone) will help you get past this fear, thereby allowing you to use this approach.

## When Your Partner Starts a Reactive Exchange

When your partner attempts to engage you in a reactive exchange, you will learn to concentrate your efforts on how not to react. You will have observed at least one way in which your partner attempts to reactively engage you, or you may have found many ways, perhaps too many. As one woman reported, "All he does is react. He's always in old brain. I don't know where to start." But you need not become dismayed if this is your situation, because everyone has only six to ten reactive, or "baiting," behaviors.

One man observed, "When I'm upset, she says 'Grow up,' and that's the point where the situation gets worse." And a woman reported, "Whenever my husband goes into a 'poor me' routine and I ask him what's wrong, the situation gets worse and he attacks me." But once you have identified your partner's baiting behavior, you will be able to plan exactly what to do to keep yourself from reacting. Your road to successful change will then follow the four stages described earlier.

Remember that when being reactive your partner is following his old brain, and is interested only in getting you to react back. When you don't react as usual, you will deprive his old brain of the reactive feedback it expects, and he will increase his provocation. While this is neither fair nor reasonable, our old brain is not concerned with such values, yet a partner's counter-reaction must not be underestimated or ignored. It can be extremely potent and come in many forms. For example, a wife describes one such provocation: "When he gets upset, he tells me about how little my mother thinks of me. Instead of attacking him back, I now tell him I don't want to hear it, but he keeps it up. When I go into the next room to get away, he follows me, still talking about my mother and me." Such counter-reactions are always best dealt with by not reacting to them. Because it's important to prepare for such opposition, you will learn how to anticipate it and work it into your plan. Plan also what you will do if your partner's efforts last for weeks or months. Your partner is not likely to give up after only one attempt on your part, but is more than likely to persist with ever more desperate provocations

In her efforts to end their cycle of reactivity, the wife of a carousing husband stopped asking him where he had been when he came home late, and he escalated by staying out still later. When she still did not inquire, he began to make noise when he returned home, thus "informing" her of how late it was. When she did not react to this, he asked her, "Don't you want to know where I've been?", as if daring her to rise to his bait. When she still did not inquire, he told their daughter that her mother was a poor wife. This cruel behavior was a quite typical old brain escalation, seeking to trigger conflict. Like an addict, this man had to have a fix, but when he is deprived of his fix often enough, the addiction will eventually cease.

Very likely, your partner will pick unexpected, inconvenient, or embarrassing times to provoke you. It may be late at night when it's inconvenient and difficult to get away, on a vacation, in front of friends or family, or when you are a long way from home. But however long your partner's efforts persist, and no matter how inconvenient the times, you can learn to be just as persistent and resourceful in not reacting back. If you do not, emotional reactivity will continue its death grip on your relationship, until every last drop of caring and happiness has been squeezed from it. Possibly three hours of inconvenience in place of three weeks or more of bad feelings is the kind of trade-off you may have to make.

During this confrontational period, it is best to refrain from trying to reason with your partner, because you will both only become more upset. You must learn to refrain even if your partner tries to keep on with the reactive exchange and does things like following you around or blocking the door if you try to leave the house. Your partner's efforts to provoke a reaction will have to subside of their own accord. Since a book cannot cover every contingency, you will need to be creative in finding ways to retreat. But remember that your partner's old brain efforts will *subside*. During this time, it is essential that you do not vent your feelings or "speak your mind" to your partner. You can do so later in a calmer and more controlled way. Then, when you are calm, it will be possible to say, "I was angry over what you did last night," without saying it in a provocatively reactive way. If your partner persists with provocation, put some physical distance between you, not as avoidance or retaliation, but in order to regain self-control. Then stay away until you are calmer. You might go into the next room, for a walk, a drive, or even to stay overnight with a friend or at a motel. Do this whenever necessary, until this opposition period has ended. And remember—*it will pass*. If you leave and your partner attacks you about having done so, it will be better than spending weeks, months, or forever trying to recover from what was said between you during the reactive infection.

To follow what has been outlined here will take a good deal of effort. But since relationship reactivity is progressive, you have only one option, which is to do something constructive to end the reactivity before it destroys your relationship completely. There is, however, no approach that will work for everyone all of the time, and this one is no exception. Some relationships cannot take the added stress that changing reactivity initially produces, and the partners may have to decide to go their separate ways. Some may find when their reactivity is reduced that they no longer care for each other—that their caring had, in fact, died a long time ago. Nevertheless, this approach has frequently been successful where all others have failed. The following comments reflect these positive changes:

We are beginning to respond, listen, and share some kindness after decades of not sharing any.

I always felt so powerless. My marriage was filled with turmoil and hostility, and I had no idea how to change it. But I've put a lot of work into it, I'm no longer helpless, and my marriage is no longer full of agitation and conflict.

We're talking about the things we used to fight about.

It's so nice now. I look forward to spending time with him rather than dreading it. We've started laughing together again, and a lot of our caring has returned. I was afraid that it was gone forever.

At first, I did all the work and he opposed me every step of the way. Then that came to a peak, and since then he's been changing faster than me. Now we both work on our problems together.

Finally, be aware that managing your reactivity will be only a first stage in repairing your relationship. The following chapters show you how to deal with defensiveness, how to communicate better once you've lessened your reactivity, and how to use your anger constructively.

## EMOTIONAL REACTIVITY WORKSHEETS

*You may wish to make several photocopies of the following pages while they are still blank, since you may be repeating these exercises several times.*

These worksheets are designed to help guide you through resolving the emotional reactivity in your life. Recording what has happened between you and your partner and custom designing a plan will help you to identify the reactivity in your relationship, as well as draining off some of these events' destructive power. As part of this process, you will "walk" through the obstacles you will most likely encounter, both within yourself and through your partner.

If you have a partner willing to cooperate with you in this process, great! You can help each other fill in your respective sheets. However, if you don't have a partner who is cooperative, or at least not yet, you can still use these worksheets, as they were designed specifically for people in your situation.

By now you will have some idea of how reactivity is affecting your own relationship, and which of your reactivity problems you would like to resolve. Write down just one goal. It is best to start with a very small goal, then when you have achieved this small goal, it will be much easier to apply what you have learned to the larger ones.

My first reactivity goal is: (For example, "I would like to be able to be in the same room as my partner without becoming upset." Or "I would like not to get into an argument while discussing our finances.")

_____

_____

_____

## OBSERVING REACTIVE ENCOUNTERS

1. It will be easier at the beginning for you to "see" your own reactive encounters after you have observed them first in others. The next time you are people-watching while shopping, at work, or with friends, see if you can identify who became reactive first, when this began, and what happened next. Describe one reactive encounter you have observed.

_____

_____

_____

Now you can begin to look at your own relationship by initially observing your partner's behaviors. The following exercises are designed with this in mind.

2. Since the switch from new to old brain reactions is where your problems begin, it is essential you pinpoint all the physiological changes you can. So first describe the physical changes in your partner's body when behaving in an old brain way. (For example, "He raises his voice." "Her eyes narrow.")

_____

_____

_____

3. Describe the physical changes in your own body when behaving in an old brain way. (For example, "My shoulders tense up.")

_____

_____

_____

4. Check the attitude changes that occur in both you and your partner when you become reactive.

| My partner becomes: | | I become: | |
| --- | --- | --- | --- |
| Unreasonable | ☐ | Unreasonable | ☐ |
| Volatile | ☐ | Volatile | ☐ |
| Uncooperative | ☐ | Uncooperative | ☐ |
| Other(s): | | | |

_____

_____

_____

5. Describe how your partner behaved during the encounter. (For example, "He spoke very cruelly to me, and afterward said he couldn't believe he had said those things.")

_____

_____

_____

6. Describe how you behaved during the reactive encounter. (For example, "After I got upset, I was not aware of what I was saying and doing until three hours later!")

_____

_____

_____

7. How long did it take for both your and your partner's new brain to resume functioning?

| My partner's resumed in: | | Mine resumed in: | |
| --- | --- | --- | --- |
| Minutes | ☐ | Minutes | ☐ |
| Hours | ☐ | Hours | ☐ |
| Days | ☐ | Days | ☐ |

8. Below, identify the triggers that have set off your partner's and your old brain. Check those which apply, and add any others you have identified.

| Partner | | Self | |
| --- | --- | --- | --- |
| A thought | ☐ | A thought | ☐ |
| An action (or lack of) | ☐ | An action (or lack of) | ☐ |
| An event outside the relationship | ☐ | An event outside the relationship | ☐ |
| A word | ☐ | A word | ☐ |
| A look | ☐ | A look | ☐ |
| A tone of voice | ☐ | A tone of voice | ☐ |
| An implication | ☐ | An implication | ☐ |
| A memory | ☐ | A memory | ☐ |
| An attitude | ☐ | An attitude | ☐ |
| An issue | ☐ | An issue | ☐ |
| Just being near the other person | ☐ | Just being near the other person | ☐ |

Other(s):

_____

_____

_____

9. Describe what you checked off above that triggers your partner's old brain. Guess as best you can if you're not sure. (For example, "He has said when I bring up our finances my voice always rises above its normal pitch.")

_____

_____

_____

10. Now describe the triggers checked above that set you off. (For example, "Whenever he raises his voice and points his finger at me I feel my blood pressure rise." "Whenever I have a difficult day at work I come home already hot.")

_____

_____

_____

## UNDERSTANDING YOUR OWN REACTIVE INFECTION

1. After you have identified your reactivity triggers, recognizing infection comes next. Once your partner is reactive describe the things your partner does that provoke *you* to react. Be specific. List tone and volume of speech, nonverbal triggers, specific words, and so on. (For example, "When he continually brings up old and sensitive topics, that's what finally sets me off.") Pay particular attention to indirect and subtle actions, such as talking through the children to get to you.

   My partner provokes me by saying/doing the following:

_____

_____

_____

2. Now do the same with yourself. Once reactive, identify clearly what you said and how you said it, that finally triggered your partner's old brain. (Was it your loaded question about his work, or the tone of what you said?)

   I provoked my partner by saying and doing the following:

_____

_____

_____

3. Once there is infection between you, the escalation is immediate. Describe what usually occurs during escalation. (For example, "We both scream and attack one another." "I become silent and sulk.")

My partner says and does the following:

_____

_____

_____

I say and do the following:

_____

_____

_____

## SEEING THE EFFECTS OF YOUR REACTIVE ENCOUNTER

1. After each reactive encounter, there are personal and relationship impacts on everyone involved. First, go down the list and check off the effects on both your partner and you.

| For Partner | | For Self | |
| --- | --- | --- | --- |
| Feeling regret | ☐ | Feeling regret | ☐ |
| Feeling upset | ☐ | Feeling upset | ☐ |
| Feeling helpless | ☐ | Feeling helpless | ☐ |
| Preoccupied | ☐ | Preoccupied | ☐ |
| Confused | ☐ | Confused | ☐ |
| Losing control | ☐ | Losing control | ☐ |
| Becoming fearful | ☐ | Becoming fearful | ☐ |
| Ashamed and embarrassed | ☐ | Ashamed and embarrassed | ☐ |
| Feeling anger and hatred | ☐ | Feeling anger and hatred | ☐ |
| Feeling frustrated | ☐ | Feeling frustrated | ☐ |
| Feeling guilty | ☐ | Feeling guilty | ☐ |
| Feeling tense | ☐ | Feeling tense | ☐ |
| Unhappy | ☐ | Unhappy | ☐ |
| Lowered self-esteem | ☐ | Lowered self-esteem | ☐ |
| Negative health effects | ☐ | Negative health effects | ☐ |
| Drawn to excessive distractions | ☐ | Drawn to excessive distractions | ☐ |

Other(s):

_____

_____

_____

2. Describe how these effects impact on your partner. (For example, "My boyfriend was clearly sad. And he drank more than usual.")

_____

_____

_____

3. Describe how these effects impact on you. (For example, "For days after I felt guilty over what I'd said. I also felt physically sick that night.")

_____

_____

_____

4. If there are others in the household, perhaps children, describe the effects of your reactive encounters on them. (For example, "They became unusually unruly." "They became withdrawn.")

_____

_____

_____

5. Now describe their effects on your relationship with others outside the home, at work, with friends, family. (For example, "I am unable to concentrate at work after one of these events.")

_____

_____

_____

6. Besides the effects on you personally, there are always relationship effects. Describe the costs they are exacting in the following areas of your relationship.

Happiness. (For example, "I no longer enjoy living with him as much as I used to. I miss this aspect of our relationship so much.")

_____

_____

Sex. (For example, "It takes me weeks to become sexually interested in her after one of these scenes.")

_____

_____

Caring. (For example, "I don't care for her as much as I used to. I can't because I have so much resentment against her.")

_____

_____

Communication. (For example, "Whenever we get reactive, we speak over one another, not hearing anything the other said, since we're too involved in presenting our own sides.")

_____

_____

Problem-solving. (For example, "When we get upset with each other, we never follow through discussing the topic we started with.")

_____

_____

7. Check off below how long these effects on your relationship last.
Hours ☐　　Days ☐　　Weeks ☐　　Months ☐
Years ☐　　They never leave ☐

Identifying the effects of emotional reactivity on your life will help sensitize you to its full impact and strengthen your motivation to eliminate it. Its deadly influence has more far-reaching effects on relationships than most people truly realize.

Don't get discouraged if you haven't filled in all the blanks. Reactive encounters will continue for some time in your relationship, and you can keep going back to fill in the blanks. But you are already a significant step closer to eliminating their life-draining influence. The next exercises will help you design and implement a plan to eliminate your reactivity.

## CONTROLLING YOUR REACTIVITY

By now you will have observed and described at least one reactive encounter that you yourself started. Here you will begin to diminish if not
eliminate these encounters entirely.

1. Describe how you act when you become reactive. (For example, "I
scream at my partner." "I become sarcastic.")
　　When I become reactive, I often say and do the following things:

_____

_____

_____

2. Describe what occurs between both of you after you become reactive. (For example, "After I provoke him into reacting, we sling the worst
mud around about the other's past.")

_____

_____

_____

3. Now plan alternatives to your own behavior that would prevent this
encounter. Very specifically, describe exactly what you will or will not say.
(For example, "I will not say she is just like her mother.")
　　The next time this occurs, I am going to say or not say the following:

_____

_____

_____

4. To maintain self-control some physical distance from your partner may
also be necessary. If so, describe how you will distance yourself. (For example, "I will go into my own room, for a walk, or a drive.")

_____

_____

_____

5. It is *imperative* that you release your negative feelings in some manner away from your partner, so that they will not ferment and resurface. List the different ways you will do so. (For example, "I will meditate, read a book, write down my feelings in a private journal, go jogging.")

After I become reactive, I will calm myself down in the following ways:

_____

_____

_____

## COPING WITH YOUR INNER OPPOSITION TO CHANGE

Very likely you will now experience a struggle between changing and not changing your behavior. This is a common occurrence, so don't feel it means that there is something wrong with you. However, I've found that when they don't expect this struggle, many people do conclude they are somehow inadequate, and they give up. One must always overcome inner resistance in order to change. (Think back to the times you tried dieting or giving up a habit. In order to succeed, you first had to find a way to "ride out" your inner resistance.) The next exercise is designed to help you identify and deal with this struggle.

1. Describe the ways your system resists your efforts not to become reactive. (For example, "I fear that I'm running from the problem." "I despair that neither this nor anything else will work.")

_____

_____

_____

Attempts to change ingrained habits rarely meet with immediate success. If you find you can't stick to your plan, that is quite normal. It will take repeated efforts for you to succeed but once you do, much less effort will be required from that point on.

You will probably find yourself going through the following phases after planning your change: forgetting to implement it, becoming aware of it during a reactive encounter, and, finally, remembering to implement it in time.

## MONITOR YOUR EFFORTS AT CHANGING BASED ON THESE FOUR STAGES.

2. Describe how it comes about that you forget what you're supposed to do when the time comes. (For example, "I completely forgot how I planned to speak to my partner. When the time came, I raised my voice like I always do. It wasn't until I calmed down that I realized how I didn't follow through on my plan.")

_____

_____

_____

Check off your attempts below.

| | | | |
|---|---|---|---|
| 1st missed opportunity | ☐ | 6th missed opportunity | ☐ |
| 2nd missed opportunity | ☐ | 7th missed opportunity | ☐ |
| 3rd missed opportunity | ☐ | 8th missed opportunity | ☐ |
| 4th missed opportunity | ☐ | 9th missed opportunity | ☐ |
| 5th missed opportunity | ☐ | 10th missed opportunity | ☐ |

Note: Don't look at these attempts as failures, but as steps which bring you closer to success.

3. Check off below whenever you were aware of your plan not to react in your usual way but you were unable to make the change.

| | | | |
|---|---|---|---|
| 1st missed opportunity | ☐ | 6th missed opportunity | ☐ |
| 2nd missed opportunity | ☐ | 7th missed opportunity | ☐ |
| 3rd missed opportunity | ☐ | 8th missed opportunity | ☐ |
| 4th missed opportunity | ☐ | 9th missed opportunity | ☐ |
| 5th missed opportunity | ☐ | 10th missed opportunity | ☐ |

4. Describe the behavior you eventually changed.

_____

_____

_____

If you've finally eliminated one source of the problems between you and your partner, congratulations, and take a break. Then start over and work on another one.

## HOW TO STOP A REACTIVE EXCHANGE BEGUN BY YOUR PARTNER

Now that you have begun to control your own reactivity, you can start to work on not reacting to your partner's. This is more difficult because your partner's reactivity will *increase* when you fail to react. The following exercises are designed to prepare you for this eventuality.

1. Describe what your partner says and does while reactive. Spell it out in exact detail, leaving out as little as possible. (For example, "When my partner comes home from work, he gets into a 'poor me' routine. When I ask him what's wrong, he whines incessantly." Or "My partner will get up in a bad mood for no apparent reason, and pick on everything I say to provoke me into arguing with her.")

_____

_____

_____

2. Now describe an alternative to your previous reactions to your partner. (For example, "The next time he begins his 'poor me' reaction, I won't ask him what's wrong." Or "When she gets up in a nasty mood, I'll avoid doing things with her that day.")

The next time my partner tries to draw me into reacting to him I will do, and not do, the following:

_____

_____

_____

3. Describe how you will use physical distance to help you accomplish this. (For example, "I'll avoid his presence by staying in another room." Or "I'll visit a friend.")

_____

_____

_____

4. If you have drawn back *after* you have reacted, you will need to calm down. List or describe here how you will calm down. (For example, "I'll read a book, work on my hobby, write in my journal.")

———————————————————————————

———————————————————————————

———————————————————————————

## COPING WITH YOUR PARTNER'S OPPOSITION

Remember, whenever our old brain is deprived of a satisfying response, it *increases* provocation. You will see this when your partner either escalates the provocation or starts using a new form of provocation, as by adding insults to the earlier sarcasm. It will be easier to cope with your partner's escalation if you can anticipate it. Below you can describe in pencil how you believe your partner will escalate, and afterward rewrite it, if it differs from what you had written.

1. Describe how this escalation tends to occur when you don't react. (For example, "When I don't ask him what's wrong, he sulks even more." Or "When I don't include him in my day's activities, he goes out of his way to call attention to the bad mood he's in.")

———————————————————————————

———————————————————————————

———————————————————————————

2. Describe how you will keep yourself from reacting to your partner's intensified provocation. (For example, "I will redouble my efforts to avoid all contact with him.")

When he increases his provocation, I will:

———————————————————————————

———————————————————————————

———————————————————————————

3. If you disengaged from your partner *after* reaching your reactive point, you did so too late. (Initially, this almost always occurs.) Describe here how you will get yourself calmer before you are together again.

_____

_____

_____

4. Frequently these escalations can last weeks or months. If you find (or believe) your partner's escalation is continuing or increasing after a week, describe how you will deal with this escalation. (For example, "If my partner follows through with his threat to never visit my family again, I will visit them without him and not plead for him to come.")

_____

_____

_____

Just as in making the original changes in behavior, very few people are initially successful at not reacting to this heightened provocation. And if this happens to you, rather than giving up, look at your failed attempts as necessary for learning. You will need to repeat such efforts or your problem will never go away. The following exercise is designed to help you move past your unsuccessful efforts.

5. You have already successfully planned your changed behavior. Now, check the times you only remembered your new response after the old brain interaction had occurred.

| | | | |
|---|---|---|---|
| 1st missed opportunity | ☐ | 6th missed opportunity | ☐ |
| 2nd missed opportunity | ☐ | 7th missed opportunity | ☐ |
| 3rd missed opportunity | ☐ | 8th missed opportunity | ☐ |
| 4th missed opportunity | ☐ | 9th missed opportunity | ☐ |
| 5th missed opportunity | ☐ | 10th missed opportunity | ☐ |

Following is a list of Do's and Don'ts that you may want to refer to occasionally.

| Do | Don't |
| --- | --- |
| Plan and mentally rehearse your new behavior. | React to provocation. Defend yourself. |
| Anticipate your partner's reactions. | Vent your feelings to your partner. |
| Vent your feelings to a friend. | Try to reason with your partner. |
| Discuss touchy issues when you both are calm. | Defend or justify what you have said. |
| Stay away from your partner until you are calm. | |
| Monitor yourself to maintain self-control. | |
| Learn from your failed attempts. | |
| Use physical distance to regain self-control. | |

6. By now you have probably become aware how not to react in your old way during an encounter, but are still unable to change. Below check the times your efforts have been unsuccessful.

| | | | |
| --- | --- | --- | --- |
| 1st missed opportunity | ☐ | 6th missed opportunity | ☐ |
| 2nd missed opportunity | ☐ | 7th missed opportunity | ☐ |
| 3rd missed opportunity | ☐ | 8th missed opportunity | ☐ |
| 4th missed opportunity | ☐ | 9th missed opportunity | ☐ |
| 5th missed opportunity | ☐ | 10th missed opportunity | ☐ |

You either have controlled or are well on the road to controlling at least one reactive encounter. Congratulations for having done one of the most difficult things you will ever do in your life!

Now return to the beginning, and repeat the process of managing another reactive behavior—both your own and your partner's.

# CHAPTER 4

# Being Defensive:

## The Illusion of Self-Protection

Learning how to restrain your emotional reactivity when you are with your partner is only part of getting along better together. In order to be close, a couple must reach a point where their significant feelings and thoughts can be communicated in a calm and undefensive environment. This chapter looks at what defensiveness really is and how to begin building a conciliatory atmosphere.

Most relationship problems are due to a few ongoing behaviors that are a source of aggravation and discontent. Being defensive is one of the ways we all cover up certain of our recurrent behaviors rather than trying to change them, and denial is one of our most common mechanisms. For example, an alcoholic may use denial rather than deal with the alcoholism, as in the following exchange.

SHE: "I don't like you when you drink. You get mean."

HE: "So now you're accusing me of being an alcoholic, right?"

SHE: "I certainly think it's possible. You fix your first drink when you come home from work, and you keep drinking until you pass out almost every night."

HE: "You're crazy! You're just in one of your moods and want to bitch about something. I work ten or twelve hours a day, and I'm under a lot of pressure. If I want to come home and have a drink or two, that's my right. And, yes, I am tired. I don't 'pass out'—I can't help it if I'm too tired to make it to bed."

Another of our common mechanisms is verbal aggression, as displayed in the following dialogue.

HE: "We really need to be spending less money. Sales aren't what they were a couple of years ago and my commission checks keep getting smaller and smaller. See what you can do to hold down expenses."

SHE: "Me! I'm not the one who runs up the credit cards! You're the one who has to have all the clothes for your big-time job! You're the one who refuses to eat leftovers or casseroles! Let's not forget that I work, too. If I see something I want once in a while, then I should have the right to buy it. Why don't you hold down *your* expenses?!"

Year after year, our defensiveness keeps us from seeing ourselves realistically, in spite of the feedback we receive about our need to change. Denial followed by attack moves the focus off ourselves and onto our partners, so that we can see their every shortcoming, and none of our own.

## Understanding Our Defensiveness

Our defensiveness is an old brain reaction. In the blink of an eye, we can go from an undefensive position (calm, reasonable, cooperative) to a defensive position (unreasonable, belligerent, uncooperative). Once we become defensive, we are unable to distinguish between a valid complaint and a hostile retaliation. Old brain thinking ignores such distinctions and sees all information as threatening and attacking. When we are in this mode, all comments are automatically dismissed as irrelevant, incorrect, or even as the ravings of a crazy person. As one woman said about her defensive partner: "Any time I say something about his behavior, he either completely ignores it or he acts like I've lost my mind and what I'm saying can't possibly be true." The distinction between true and false messages is of vital importance here. If what is said is *not* true, then ignoring it is a valid and reasonable response, but if what is said *is* true, the consequences of ignoring it are severe.

Like a reflex reaction to criticism, defensiveness occurs before we can make an objective evaluation of its truthfulness. By automatically dismissing a criticism, it tries to protect us from immediate emotional discomfort. But it also keeps us from making much-needed changes and produces far-reaching negative consequences.

Our defensiveness sets off an internal alarm to alert the old brain to a perceived challenge, such as when we hear information that contradicts what we wish to believe about ourselves. When this happens, our tension level increases, our defenses click on, and we instantly react against whatever was said. For example, as was said about this woman: "She's so defensive, she doesn't hear a word I say! I get so frustrated I feel like strangling her!" Often, when we are firmly entrenched in our old brain, all further outside information is automatically deflected, and we "mis-hear" what follows. Perhaps we unconsciously assume things which have not been said, as was described in this example: "All I said was 'Please turn down the television,' and he was off on a tirade about me having said he was lazy!" Or our listening stops altogether, as in this relationship: "I tell her she looks good all the time, but when I said that I didn't like her dress, she accused me of never saying anything nice about her!" Thus, interpretations and assumptions are made that support what our old brain wants to hear rather than what was actually said. If some information *was* taken in, it is explained away, simply denied, or the subject is changed.

After this has happened we begin a counterattack and reactive infection takes place. This is immediately followed by escalation in the form of a reciprocal counterattack. All discussion has ceased and is replaced by argument in which we each mindlessly attack the other, and blindly defend ourselves. Charges may be hurled back and forth, the past dredged up, cutting or hurting remarks made, name-calling may escalate, and so on. From this point on, all communication (and contact) is destructive, and what may have begun as a simple comment or discussion has quickly turned into an argument triggered by one's defensiveness. (How not to get trapped in defending yourself is discussed further in chapter 5.)

## The High Cost of Defensiveness

There is always a cost for reacting defensively. It stops effective communication, prevents problem-solving, and depletes caring. As a result, the quality of both partners' lives deteriorates. Like all reactive behavior, once it has begun it inevitably worsens. As one person confided, "I've been defensive so long, I don't even realize I'm doing it any more, much less know how to stop it."

Because defensiveness keeps us from learning from our mistakes, we tend to repeat them. The overbearing wife continues being overbearing, the spiteful husband continues being spiteful, and the inattentive lover continues to be inattentive. Defensively protecting their behavior, and unable to see themselves realistically, they retain the false hope that they will be able to escape the consequences. The following example illustrates this situation.

A couple who attended marriage counseling had been married for nine years before separating for a year and then trying to get back together. Their problems had centered primarily on the same issues throughout most of their marriage. For years the husband railed against his wife's dependence on her parents. She went to them with her marital problems without having first talked to her husband, and this always led to her parents' intrusion into their problems. In addition, his wife constantly sided with the children against him, and he felt she was undermining his authority. The wife railed against the husband because she was left totally responsible for paying their bills and raising the children.

Throughout their marriage, each time one commented on the other's behavior, it was dismissed defensively and responded to with countercharges, as they each defended their own behavior instead of considering the comment's validity. If only one of them had listened to what was being said and corrected it, it would have gone a long way toward resolving many of their problems. Instead, they endured years of bitter fights and allowed their mutual caring to die, all the while falsely hoping they could get away with not changing. As always happens, the consequences of their self-deception eventually caught up with them, and it became intolerable to live together. Subsequently, both partners still had to face changing their behavior, as well as trying to rekindle their mutual caring.

During their year of separation, they did much reflecting and soul searching, and each came to see the validity of what the other had been saying. She realized that she was, indeed, too dependent on her parents and that the children ignored or were disrespectful to their father because she always intervened on their behalf. He, in turn, realized that he was not carrying enough responsibility for the children and around the house in general. The "truth" each had believed about themselves was not so accurate after all. In the husband's own words: "All these years of resentment and argument have been for nothing. Much of it could have been prevented if either of us had just listened to what the other was saying."

Being able to recognize and accept a criticism as valid is essential to relationship harmony.

## Using Your Defensiveness Constructively

All defensiveness is reactive, provoking an immediate response, which usually results in argument, emotional turmoil, and bad feelings—never in anything positive. And this destructive cycle will continue in our relationship until one of us reduces our defensiveness. Contrary to what is generally believed, our real power for ending this destructive cycle lies in lessening our own defensiveness, and decreasing the number of arguments we ourselves provoke.

### Identifying Defensiveness
Mutual defensiveness invariably contributes to discord between partners. So the more readily you can recognize what is described here as it happens in your relationship, the better you will be able to eliminate its contribution to your own problems. The first step is to raise your awareness. Because it is a form of old brain behavior, when

we become defensive we lose much of our self-awareness. At first it may be easier to observe how defensiveness operates in others, outside our own relationships, for example, when our married friends talk to each other. This should be relatively easy, since it plays a big part in all relationships experiencing problems. Then, after you have observed it in others, you will be able to begin to concentrate on observing it in your partner. The worksheets at the end of this chapter will help you see which subjects are triggers for your partner's defensiveness and how your partner becomes defensive when you point out any inconsistencies, excuses, or evasions. You will notice your partner's physiological reactions to sensitive subjects. One person's eyes may widen and the face flush, another's voice pitch may rise and its volume increase, and often one's body becomes rigid and fists are clenched. These all signal a defensive reaction.

Finally, you will be able to use this information to unravel your own defensive mechanisms, because this is where your real power for improvement lies. In the worksheets, you can apply what is described here to dissect your recent reactive exchanges. You will note your own physiological changes when your more sensitive triggers are tripped. You will look back at what happened to see the events and yourself more clearly and to decipher the mechanisms that you use to dismiss information, regardless of its validity. You will learn to observe indirect clues from those around you about your own behavior and to pay particular attention to them. Many people may offer feedback in the more roundabout form of digs, sarcasm, or side comments. As one man finally realized, "My colleagues at work have been telling me the same thing my wife has been telling me. I'd never noticed before what they were saying."

In our intimate relationships, indirect comments can have as powerful an effect as direct ones. Our violent reactions to indirect (or misheard) comments are often due to our having already suspected that we were in the wrong. Criticisms can also be expressed through "family jokes." One husband described this: "For years my wife called me her 'favorite couch potato.' Even though she would say it lovingly, it made me mad, and then I would sit, sulk, and watch TV. The more she said it, the more I sulked, and it became a downward spiral."

Of course, it is much easier to observe defensiveness in someone other than yourself, but the more you can confront your own short-comings (rather than your partner's), the better off you will both be, ultimately. If you let yourself, you will be able to observe the struggle inside you between the part that wants to look at what was said to you and the part that wants to continue to overlook it. Try to accept that there will be pain when you start coming to terms with the truth of what is being said to you, and remember that you will benefit in the long run.

As you already know, while it is easier in the short run to ignore one's shortcomings than to admit to them, what will happen in the long run is more important. This struggle was described by one young woman in this way:

> For years I allowed myself to be negatively influenced by my friends. My partner kept telling me that, but I ignored it. When I finally 'heard' it and changed, I not only got rid of their bad advice, but also of an ongoing problem that had cost me much happiness. Admitting this to myself was the most difficult part.

## Mastering Your Own Defensiveness

While many people admit to being defensive, they expect their partners to learn to live with it so that they will not have to make any changes. But the accompanying hope that their situation will improve in spite of their behavior or other relationship conflicts is a false hope. Instead, the problems will continue and nothing will be gained. Whenever you are being defensive, the responsibility rests with you to do something about it. And since our defensiveness acts as an instant catalyst for argument, it must be restrained before it is triggered. Before you succeed, you will have to go through the stages mentioned earlier of first identifying your old behavior and planning a new one, then forgetting about it while in the midst of a reactive interaction, then becoming increasingly aware of what you want to do differently the next time, until finally you will be able to carry it out successfully. You will undoubtedly go through an inner struggle, as part of you will fight to continue your old behavior, and another part will fight to change it. Your readiness to learn from your missed opportunities will be crucial to your relationship's improvement.

## Self-Evaluation

Reducing your own defensiveness is half the battle, though perhaps the easy half. Next, you must begin to evaluate the criticism's validity. While this may sound easy, it is very painful to do. It will feel emotionally *and* physically repugnant to admit that what was said to you may indeed be valid, especially after many years of having denied it. But repugnant or not, if you truly want your life and relationship to improve, it is something that has to be done. The cost of not doing so is the continuation of the problems that undermine your relationship. Once again, the harder you try to confront your own shortcomings, rather than your partner's, the more your life and relationship will improve.

It is often difficult to know whether what you are told is valid or invalid. Your partner may be criticizing your behavior because she is mad about something that happened earlier in the day that had nothing to do with you. But then again, the criticism may be accurate. If what was said is true and you dismiss it as false, any problems generated by your own behavior will continue. On the other hand, if it is not accurate, try to look at it for what it is—a way of blowing off steam—and ignore the "information." To help you evaluate the truth of what your partner is saying, you can use the cues your own body gives you, remembering that we frequently react the most strongly to comments we suspect are true. It is best to do your evaluating after the discussion has ended and you are calmer.

You can also run your partner's comments by others, such as friends, co-workers, or family members. For example, one woman whose husband told her she was moody found that her co-workers confirmed this. Upon reflection, she decided that there was some truth in it and she wanted to make a change. On the other hand, you may find what your partner tells you too difficult to talk about to others. If this happens, digest as much as you can at your own pace, observing it over time. Whenever this kind of criticism gets through, you can't help but take it to heart. Some people will feel a sharp pain in the pit of their stomach because they are experiencing a direct attack on their self-deception. However, do not let this experience keep you from discovering the validity of what is being said. Once you have learned to absorb a valid criticism, you will be able to put your pain to constructive use. Use it as a sign that you may be avoiding something that you do not want to face, rather than simply continuing to blame your partner for this hurt. As one man said about this process, "Now, when I feel that knife in my stomach after someone makes a comment about me, I use it to stop and reflect on what was said. Before, I automatically reacted to the hurt by blasting whoever said it."

If a criticism was accurate, the fastest way to get over your pain is to start working on changing the criticized behavior. Once you succeed, you will not have to listen to the criticism any more. Be as honest with yourself as you can, and stay alert for signs of your own rigidity and unreasonableness. Observe, listen, and reflect, rather than automatically dismissing, blaming, or attacking the "messenger." A father described his experience: "I never realized the children had so many problems with the way I treated them. I always ignored their complaints. Now that I'm admitting to myself that what they say may be true, I've changed, and we're getting along much better."

Remember that feedback from others will come in many different forms, such as in sarcasm or jokes, all of which can be turned to your advantage if you listen. Using your defensiveness and sensitivities as a way to discover your own shortcomings will have a very powerful effect on both your marriage and life in general. And if you find it too difficult to verbally acknowledge the change you know you must make, you can still strive to change the problem behavior.

The following comments reflect some common reactions to this difficult process of self-change. (The worksheets that follow them will guide you through the steps of decreasing your defensiveness.)

The easy part was controlling my defensiveness. The part I struggled with most was admitting to myself and my partner that what he was saying was true. How I agonized over that!

Now I listen rather than argue when he makes a comment about me, weigh what is said, and then change if I find I have been wrong. At the beginning, this was extremely difficult to do. I took everything personally and ripped him to shreds no matter what he said about me.

My main focus has always been on getting my wife to be less defensive so that she could hear what I was saying to her. When I started concentrating on myself, I found how defensive I was too, and how difficult it is to stop (although I expected her to stop it just like that). But most important, I realized how much I could improve our relationship by making changes in myself.

## DEFENSIVENESS WORKSHEETS

*You may wish to make several photocopies of the following pages while they are still blank, since you may be repeating these exercises several times.*

The following worksheets are designed to help you identify and then eliminate the problems your own defensiveness is causing in your relationship. These exercises are not meant to be completed in one sitting. Some or perhaps many lines will be left blank. As you know, self-analysis cannot be accomplished all at once. It will be more important to use your ongoing reactive encounters as opportunities to add to this type of self-knowledge. So don't lose heart if you have to leave empty spaces. They were left in my own pages too.

## HOW TO IDENTIFY YOUR PARTNER'S DEFENSIVENESS

Because defensiveness is an old brain behavior, when we act in this manner we lose much if not all awareness that we are being defensive. This first set of exercises is designed to help you heighten your awareness.

As mentioned earlier, it is easier to identify our own defensiveness if we can first observe it in other people's lives.

1. Describe a reactive encounter that was set off by someone's defensiveness. (For example, "I was at a friend's when he and his girlfriend got into an argument; he got upset and defensive over a simple comment she made about the weather.") You can do this kind of people-watching anywhere.

_____

_____

_____

2. Now start to describe your own partner's defensiveness. Check where she showed that she was becoming defensive:

Face (eyes, skin changing color) ☐    Voice (tone, pitch, volume) ☐
Body posture, gesture ☐
Other(s) ☐

3. Describe these changes here. (For example, "His voice gets louder.")

_____

_____

_____

4. List the topics your partner gets defensive over. (For example, money, children, work.)

_____

_____

_____

5. Below is a list of defensive mechanisms. Check those that apply to your partner.

| | | | |
|---|---|---|---|
| Mishearing | ☐ | Ignoring | ☐ |
| Distorting | ☐ | Not hearing | ☐ |
| Rationalizing | ☐ | Making excuses | ☐ |
| Misinterpreting | ☐ | Evading | ☐ |
| Changing the subject | ☐ | Lying | ☐ |
| Justifying | ☐ | Attacking | ☐ |

Sulking/withdrawing          ☐          Denying                              ☐
Other(s)

_____

Describe these mechanisms here. (For example, "She made excuses for everything said.")

_____

_____

_____

6. Describe the effect of the above on you and on your relationship. (For example, "After ten years, her defensiveness on the topic of her mother bothers me so much I can't see straight, and I deeply resent her.")

_____

_____

_____

## HOW TO IDENTIFY YOUR OWN DEFENSIVENESS

You now have an idea of how your partner's defensiveness works, as well as the problems it creates. If you believe your partner will be open to this information, do share it. However, if you believe it will only provoke a defensive response, *do not* share it! You will learn how to get past your partner's defensiveness in the following chapters. These worksheets aim to help you eliminate your own defensiveness.

The following set of exercises will help you identify your own defensive reactions. To help you fill in these next worksheets, look back at your past reactive encounters.

1. Start by listing the physical changes you experience when you become defensive. (For example, Your heart speeds up; you feel knots in your stomach.)

_____

_____

_____

2. Describe any changes in your attitude when you become defensive. (For example, you move from calm to belligerent or reasonable to unreasonable.)

_____

_____

_____

3. Note any changes in your manner of speech.

Tone ☐ Volume ☐

Speed of your words ☐

Other(s)

_____

_____

_____

4. List the subjects of discussion around which these reactive changes occur. (For example, the house's appearance, your weight.)

_____

_____

_____

5. Now check off which of the following defensive mechanisms apply to you.

| | | | |
|---|---|---|---|
| Mishearing | ☐ | Ignoring | ☐ |
| Distorting | ☐ | Not hearing | ☐ |
| Rationalizing | ☐ | Making excuses | ☐ |
| Misinterpreting | ☐ | Evading | ☐ |
| Changing the subject | ☐ | Lying | ☐ |
| Justifying | ☐ | Attacking | ☐ |
| Sulking/withdrawing | ☐ | Denying | ☐ |

Other(s)

_____

_____

_____

6. Fully describe how and when you do these things. (For example, "Whenever he comments on my parents, I make excuses why they behaved as they did, then I attack *his* parents.")

_____

_____

_____

7. Fill in how long it takes for a reactive exchange to occur between you and your partner once you become defensive.

Seconds □          Minutes          □
Other

_____

_____

Describe the effect your defensiveness has on you and the relationship. (For example, "I end up very tense and things are strained between us all day.")

_____

_____

_____

If you have left any blank spaces, don't be discouraged. This is to be expected. Simply go back and try to fill them in after you have had another defensive reaction. The important thing is not to give up.

## MASTERING YOUR OWN DEFENSIVENESS

The following exercises are designed to help you eliminate your own defensive reactions.

1. From the above list of checked-off defenses, pick the one you want to control first. Describe how you react when a sensitive issue triggers this form of defensiveness. (For example, "Whenever the subject of the children comes up, I withdraw and sulk.")

_____

_____

_____

2. Now describe what you will do instead. (For example, "This time when the subject of my son is raised, instead of changing the subject I will remain quiet.")

_____

_____

_____

_____

Initially, don't aim to accomplish too much. A small behavior change, as in the example above, is a good first step.

## HANDLING YOUR UNSUCCESSFUL ATTEMPTS

Before successfully changing your behavior, like most people you will go through the four stages of change discussed previously. The first stage—planning your change—you have completed.

1. In the second stage you will forget your planned change when the opportunities arise. (For example, you snapped at your partner again instead of not responding at all, as planned.) Check off each of your unsuccessful attempts.

| | | | |
|---|---|---|---|
| 1st missed opportunity | ☐ | 6th missed opportunity | ☐ |
| 2nd missed opportunity | ☐ | 7th missed opportunity | ☐ |
| 3rd missed opportunity | ☐ | 8th missed opportunity | ☐ |
| 4th missed opportunity | ☐ | 9th missed opportunity | ☐ |
| 5th missed opportunity | ☐ | 10th missed opportunity | ☐ |

2. In the third stage you will remain aware of the change you want to make, but will be unable to make it. (For example, you will be aware of not wanting to snap at your partner, but will be unable to restrain yourself.) Check off your attempts to change.

| | | | |
|---|---|---|---|
| 1st missed opportunity | ☐ | 6th missed opportunity | ☐ |
| 2nd missed opportunity | ☐ | 7th missed opportunity | ☐ |
| 3rd missed opportunity | ☐ | 8th missed opportunity | ☐ |
| 4th missed opportunity | ☐ | 9th missed opportunity | ☐ |
| 5th missed opportunity | ☐ | 10th missed opportunity | ☐ |

3. In the fourth stage, you do make a successful change. Describe your change here. (For example, "I used to sulk and not talk to my partner for the rest of the week. Now I can at least stay in the same room with him and engage in small talk.")

_____

_____

If you are interested in moving beyond changing your behavior to evaluating the validity of any criticisms you have received, continue. If not, please go on to the next chapter.

## EVALUATING YOURSELF

Your battle is half over. You have reduced or eliminated at least one of your defensive reactions. The short-term problems triggered by this particular reaction are over. Now you have resolved to evaluate the validity of the criticism you received. The following exercises are geared toward helping you evaluate their validity. For most people this is a very painful thing to do, but it is essential if you wish to significantly improve your relationship over the long term. That you have decided to undertake this task shows your strong commitment to improving your relationship.

1. Record what your partner is saying about you. (For example, "He says I am being overprotective with the children.")

_____

_____

_____

2. Can you reflect on what was said about you as possibly being true, or do you immediately dismiss it? Check one.
I automatically dismiss it    ☐        I reflect on its validity        ☐

3. If it were true, what would hurt most about it? (For example, "I would feel like a failure." "My pride would be wounded.")

_____

_____

4. Do you feel an inner struggle between wanting to look at the criticism and avoiding looking at it? Check one.

Yes ☐ No ☐

If you answered yes, describe this struggle. (For example, "Part of me says to forget it, he's just being foolish. Another part says he may be right and I need to stop being so stubborn. It hurts to think that what he has been saying about me may be true.")

_____

_____

_____

5. Describe how you will evaluate the accuracy of the criticism. (For example, "I will talk to two friends about it, and also observe myself over time to see if it is accurate.")

_____

_____

_____

6. If the criticism is valid, what effect will *not* changing the behavior continue to have on the relationship and your life? (For example, "If the criticism is true, I will continue to provoke arguments, keep us from being closer and damage my relationship with the children.")

_____

_____

_____

7. If the criticism is valid, what effect *will* changing the behavior have on your relationship and your life? (For example, "It will allow us to enjoy more of our time together, remove some of my own resentment and strengthen the family.")

_____

_____

_____

8. If you now believe the criticism of you is true, please fill in the following.

Since the criticism is true I will have to (for example, "learn how to stop making excuses for the children's behavior and hold them accountable for their actions"):

_____

_____

_____

If you've come this far, you've done exceptionally well! Be aware that defensiveness can resurface and can occur around many different issues. Over time, go back and keep applying these worksheets to other defensive reactions until your defensiveness has been totally eliminated.

# CHAPTER 5

# Togetherness:

## Balancing "I" and "We"

The traditional, widely accepted view of couple togetherness is that it begins when a man and woman stop thinking of themselves as individuals ("he," "she," "you," and "I"), and start thinking of themselves in terms of "we" and "us." This change of identity leads to a deeper companionship and greater sharing, as well as to greater tenderness and a heightened awareness of one another. In addition, it instills a sense of belonging, a greater feeling of security, and a sense of being appreciated and cared about. However, it can also create an ongoing struggle between personal and joint identity, between retaining individuality and yet giving it up for the togetherness of a relationship. The ideal balance is for the partners to develop an ability to act together as well as apart, and to feel part of a "we" without feeling they are giving up their individuality and uniqueness.

Many couples with problems meet this struggle by focusing exclusively on togetherness. They believe that both partners (and everyone else in the family) must think alike and share the same opinions, values, beliefs, and feelings on every issue. Such a belief frequently develops during courtship when differences are glossed over as unimportant and similarities are overemphasized. For example, in the interest of togetherness, neither looks at the fact that he likes Bach and Beethoven and she likes rock 'n' roll. But regardless of whether or not differences are overlooked, two individuals, each with different and inescapable opinions, beliefs, values, feelings, and thoughts, have come together. The key word is "inescapable." Yet many partners attempt to deny or suppress their innate differences, forcing similarity where none exists. When this happens, the benefits gained from expressing a variety of views, values, beliefs, and interests are lost. Equally unfortunate is the tension that can develop whenever differences are expressed, leading at worst to arguments and conflict.

The source of such conflicts becomes clearer upon examining how we understand the concept of agreement. The dictionary refers to it as "the act of agreeing or coming to a mutual arrangement." Compromise, on the other hand, is defined as "to adjust or settle by partial or mutual relinquishment of principles, position, or claim." When a couple is experiencing problems, their struggle over agreement and compromise becomes a quest for sameness of thought and identity, rather than an attempt to define, appreciate, and respect mutual differences. Then, when agreement on an opinion, belief, value, or feeling cannot be reached, the goal becomes compromise. Here either one partner gives in (at least on the surface) so as to adopt a similar opinion or both abdicate their positions to accept a compromise in which neither one truly believes.

## Competing for Rightness

Prior to their marriage, each partner thought it was acceptable to have different opinions about someone or something (he could go home and listen to classical music, and she to jazz). Expressing these differences encouraged discussion and sharing. Based on their musical differences, with neither one criticizing the other, they were able to express openly the emotions and sensations evoked by their personal tastes. However, once each believes that there can be only a right or a wrong opinion, a win/lose rivalry begins. No longer sharing with each other, the partners begin competing against one another. One partner clearly expressed this: "We no longer share our opinions. It is more like we compete for the right one!" Ironically, both are striving for a goal they can never achieve, since they are treating subjective opinions as if they were objective facts. While who won an election is a matter of fact, whether or not that person will be successful is a matter of personal opinion and conjecture. But sometimes such seemingly clear lines become fuzzy. That a man comes home inebriated is a matter of fact. But whether or not he has the right to do so is a matter of opinion. Even whether he is "drunk" can be a matter of opinion. If he passes out in the front yard, it is pretty clear he is drunk. But if he comes in, watches television for a while, and then falls asleep in his chair, his sobriety can be a matter of opinion.

Competition for rightness leads to battles for superiority— which view is better, which opinion is correct, which feeling is more valid—each trying to force opinions on the other. One woman said that when she did not agree with her husband he would say, "You're entitled to your opinions and I'm entitled to my facts." Unhappily, such implied criticisms tend to produce such retaliations as sulking, nagging, or a full counterattack.

The calm and open sharing of differing values, opinions, beliefs, feelings, and ideas during courtship is lost when this right/wrong competition begins. Instead, expressions of differences are taken as personal criticisms, pushing each partner into a reactive position with its ensuing conflict. Real communication ends as they both attack each other's opinions and defend their own. Often this is followed by a debate over who was at fault for "starting" the resulting disagreement. What used to be an enriching discussion has become a frustrating and stress-filled battle of one-upmanship. For couples with problems, this pattern tends to repeat year after year and over the same issues. As one young woman said, "We used to talk about so many things. Now if we were to talk about these same things, in a few minutes we'd be mad at one another for the rest of the month." Winning the argument has become the only issue of importance.

Though such efforts at forcing agreement affect many different aspects of a relationship, they especially affect communication. For some, it means no longer expressing their true feelings, because doing so would leave them open to attack or ridicule. But this in turn leads to resentment and, as one man said, "I feel like I don't matter. My whole marriage I've agreed with everything my wife has said. Now I feel like a nobody."

It can also profoundly affect how people feel about themselves. A woman related: "I had an unplanned pregnancy, and my husband told me he didn't want any more kids, and wanted me to get an abortion. I consider abortion murder but, like always, I agreed with him to keep the peace. Now, three years later, I still can't live with what I did." But once a partner starts agreeing with the other for the sake of togetherness, the problem arises of when and how to stop doing so, as well as what the repercussions of stopping will be. Along with the spurious feeling of togetherness provided by forced agreement, eventually there will also be increased reactivity and spoiled communication, pushing the partners still further apart.

## Expressing Your True Self

Our identity, our self, is a synthesis of everything we are: what we feel, think, and do on every level. It is the sum of our uniqueness, with all our goals, beliefs, values, and interests. It is our true "I." In our relationships, it is important to be able to differentiate this true "I" from a reactive "I" position. This difference is subtle yet crucial. True "I" positions come from our new brain, and involve searching our soul and weighing all factors as best we can. They do not come in reaction to, or in order to get a reaction out of, our partner. They are also not to be confused with stubbornness, because a true "I" position means remaining open to new information and input from others. "I" statements are never made to defy, hurt, spite, placate, manipulate, or intimidate the other person, or to defend oneself; nor are they made in fear, to gain the other's approval or permission. Since making true "I" statements is an action rather than a reaction, it does not provoke retaliatory reactive remarks. Instead, it will defuse tense and reactive topics and keep the lines of communication open. In contrast, reactive "I" positions represent an assumed self, where an opinion, belief, value, or feeling is taken on primarily to defend, defy, attack, manipulate, justify, hurt, intimidate, retaliate, or placate for approval. Such expressions provoke defensive reactivity, and will start an argument or continue one that has already begun.

Differences in opinions, interests, goals, and feelings can be expected in any intimate relationship. Because of this, every couple perpetually faces the question of how they are going to handle their differences. *Not* facing these differences is not a realistic option. I see couples who are experiencing problems deal with their differences either by denying them and acting as though they don't exist or by emphasizing and quarreling over them.

Most partners do express their differences at the beginning of their relationships, but if doing so creates problems, they eventually avoid expressing them. There is another option, however, and that is learning how to express personal differences without fighting over them. A young husband put it best when he said, "We have to learn to disagree with one another without being disagreeable about it." Once again, this sounds easier than it really is, and there is always more involved than simply expressing a true opinion. Most importantly, there is often the difficulty of dealing with a partner's attack on that opinion.

## Not Defending Against Attack

As discussed in the chapter on reactivity, it might not be what we do that stops an attack but rather what we don't do. Typically, we defend or justify, explain over and over, plead for understanding, approval, or permission (as when we say, "Please don't get mad when I say..."), or we counterattack. But the key to resolving this problem is learning to express our opinions while not defending ourselves against attack. It's true that when we are attacked, a normal reaction is to defend ourselves. But even though such a reaction is normal, it is still a reactive response, and it will make the situation worse. Thus, one partner's attacks start an argument, and the other's defense continues it. In this way, both contribute equally to the situation, and real communication stops. One woman described this: "Once I start defending myself against his attacks, whatever I wanted to say doesn't get said because I'm too busy defending myself." As in other reactive exchanges, problem-solving ceases, caring is diminished, and there are heavy personal costs, such as loss of self-respect.

After a defensive pattern of communication has been started in your relationship, it will worsen if it is not dealt with appropriately. And the resolution of this issue will come from learning how to express yourself without defending against attack, no matter how relentless. Once you have learned how to do this, you will be able to keep the lines of communication open for improvement. (Note that the issues of blame and responsibility in a relationship are discussed in the next chapter.)

Most people approach learning to express their true selves with the assumption that their partners must actively cooperate with them, not attacking them, criticizing, becoming angry or hurt, or thinking badly of them. But the reality is that at first, your partner will not approve of your efforts but will give you a hard time and become angry, feel hurt, pout, retaliate, think ill of you, and probably attempt to sabotage your efforts. As we know only too well, all change is uncomfortable, and we all fight to avoid it. You will need to maintain your position in spite of this opposition, rather than expecting it to quickly melt away.

In dealing with this issue, one person alone can create an atmosphere where differences will at least be tolerated, and at best will enrich both lives. The rest of this chapter and the worksheets that follow will help guide you toward this goal. You will learn to move your relationship away from forced agreement or open warfare toward a cooperative pattern that respects your mutual differences. Ultimately, you will both be able to feel and say, "It is O.K. if we're different." And this will come about if you learn how to express your view without defending yourself or attacking your partner, no matter how persistently you are being attacked. Eventually your partner will learn to reciprocate.

## Observing Your Disagreements

With the help of the worksheets you will first learn to sharpen your perception by identifying the areas where intolerance of your differences is creating problems between you and your partner. When you have done so, you will discover some clarity in the seemingly confusing and hopeless jumble of events. As before, it may be easier to observe this process initially in other people, such as friends or even strangers that you overhear. But when you are looking at yourself, you can start by looking back on a recent reactive exchange or observing new ones as they develop.

By looking at your communication, you can observe when and how your partner competes with you over viewpoints and makes the discussion one of right and wrong, win or lose. As one man observed, "She doesn't say, 'This is what I think.' Instead, she leaves it as if it's the only correct opinion, and that everyone thinks, or should think, this way."

You will also discover that the more tense the situation becomes, the more reactive your dialogue becomes. After you have observed your partner, switch your focus, applying what you observed in your partner to yourself. Notice how difficult it becomes to make and stick to true "I" statements as you become more tense and angry. Learn to observe yourself when your partner disagrees with you. Notice how you then feel compelled to satisfy your old brain urge for retaliation and how punishing your partner for being different from you seems to become almost second nature. Yet in reality, no victory can come from intimidating someone into agreeing with you. You can only succeed in proving that you can yell louder, pout longer, or be more sarcastic than someone else. On the other hand, a great deal of agony comes with giving up your position in order to placate your partner. If you lie either to yourself or your partner about who you really are, both you and your relationship will suffer.

Considering these things should increase your motivation to change your reactions to disagreement with your partner. Admitting that differences of opinion make you feel insecure is the first step to becoming more secure about this. It is the source of all other improvement. The key to success lies in confronting yourself and in not confronting your partner. "Seeing" your interactions differently will take time, so keep looking at any unclear situations until they become clearer. You can turn the tension and disagreements in your relationship to your advantage by letting them alert you to the source of your problems. If you keep examining your reactive exchanges, a pattern will become clear. One man who did this said, "All these years, I would say I agreed with my wife when I really didn't. At the same time, I wondered why I felt such resentment against someone with whom I saw eye-to-eye on so many issues. Now that I know why, I can do something about it."

When it is too difficult to understand what is happening during an exchange, you can try to trace the reactive events back to their source. A young married woman did this and reported, "On further thought, it became clear that it started when he said he wanted to visit Williamsburg, Virginia, with or without me, and I said, 'Why would anyone want to see old buildings?' It was my attack on his interest, which differed from mine, that started our argument."

You can use what you learn about your differences as a tool to resolve problems in your relationship if you keep in mind that your exchanges are reactive. Know that your relationship will get worse if these things are not addressed and that when one partner begins the work of understanding what triggers disagreements, improvements begin for both.

## Respecting Your Partner's Differentness

We naturally want our opinions listened to, supported and respected, but unfortunately, it is equally human to criticize those that differ from ours. In addressing this issue, you will learn how to stop pressuring, attacking, or somehow punishing your partner for differing from you. Then, after having identified the circumstances that cause you to attack your partner, you will learn to discover what you can do differently and how to go about it step by step. You can practice your new behavior in your head or with a friend, in the exact sequence you want, doing it over and over until you feel you have mastered it. Since this approach will be new to you, you will experience an inner resistance to such a change, and your anti-change forces will continue to see your partner's differences as a personal affront. You may feel hurt and insulted, angry, or betrayed. As one young husband put it, "I have trouble keeping myself from attacking her opinion, even when I've asked her for it."

## *Using Your Pain and Anger Constructively*

Though you will feel like expressing your negative feelings to your partner, it is imperative you do not do so at this time. You will be in a tense and reactive time in your relationship, and venting these feelings will only increase your mutual reactivity, with painful results. The time will come when these feelings will lessen significantly, you will feel more in control, and what is left to express can be vented. Long-lasting improvement in any relationship comes more from changing negative behavior than from expressing negative feelings. If you want to confront someone about the painful predicament you are in, it will be more constructive to confront yourself rather than your partner. And if you feel you must vent your negative feelings somehow, vent them with a friend, or go away by yourself in your car and shout at your partner there. Following through on any personal change always takes a good deal of effort. You can redirect your angry energy to supply you with the strength you will need to follow through with change, rather than directing it at your partner. So do get angry, even very angry, but redirect that anger to transform it into constructive action.

You will need to learn also from your unsuccessful attempts at changing your reactions to your differences. You will do so in the worksheets by examining what happened between you, then replanning and trying again, inching ever closer toward eliminating your own reactivity in this area. You do not need to like or respect your partner's differing from you, though that will come much later. At this stage, all you need to do is stop attacking it. Be aware that even though you are giving your partner room to be different, your partner will not automatically do the same for you. Instead, your partner may at first oppose your changes. This common reaction was accurately described: "When I stopped attacking her views, to my surprise she attacked whatever I expressed even more!"

*Making True "I" Statements*

Many people believe they hold certain views, when in fact they are expressing these views only to force their partners into agreement or to provoke them. To discover if your position is a true expression of what you really think, feel, believe, and value, you will have to scrutinize yourself very closely. Being able to offer your true "I" position is absolutely essential if you are hoping to open up communication with your partner and become closer to each other again. Reactive statements will, without exception, provoke reactivity. The old saying "Never answer an angry word with an angry word—it is the second word that makes the quarrel" is very applicable here. An equally important reason to share your true "I" position is that it is an expression of your own identity and uniqueness. If you want to be known and loved for who you really are, you must let others know you truthfully. And finally, a true "I" statement will defuse rather than inflame a tense situation.

## Dealing with Your Own Inner and Your Partner's Opposition

You will need to learn how to express your opinion as a subjective view, rather than as an absolute truth. And to do so, you will need to deal with your inner conflict. Part of you will want to express yourself in this new way, and another part will fight against it. When this struggle surfaces, you may feel afraid that your partner will dislike you if you express your true belief, or will be angry at you, or will feel hurt because you are disagreeing. You may feel guilty, undecided, or confused. Then you will also have to face your partner's opposition. Because you have upset an emotionally familiar and complacent world, your partner will initially oppose your efforts and try to shift your relationship back to its former competitive pattern. This was summed up well in one woman's experience: "After years of not giving my opinion, I finally gave it to him. Although he always said he wanted to know what I really thought, when he finally heard it, he got mad and immediately attacked it."

Your own partner's efforts may take the form of baiting, accusations, and retaliation, or trying to lure you into defending your opinion as if it were wrong, so that then his "must" be right. But, of course, there can be no right or wrong opinions, since they are based only on the information available to us, balanced with our own desires and expectations. Here, too, it will be important to work your partner's covert or overt escalation into your plan. This will be your "make or break" point, and it is also the most frequent failure point. Eventually, you must learn not to succumb to your partner's attacks and not to defend your own position.

You may worry that you will never be heard, but ultimately you will be. In fact, you will be more likely to be heard than if you continue to defend yourself with reactive retorts. When you find yourself under attack, concentrate on not defending your opinion; simply state your view and say *nothing more*. Do not explain why you feel this way, or answer your partner's charges, or try to reason with or persuade him. Nothing more needs to be said or done. Also, do not justify what you have said, seek permission or approval to say it, or attack your partner in return when your comments provoke further attack. What will succeed is your *not* doing any of these things. Hard as it is to accept, your opinion is neither more nor less valid than your partner's. It is simply a statement of what you think, feel, or believe. Even an issue as sensitive as religion is still based only on opinion.

To succeed, you will have to monitor yourself very closely, remembering that as soon as you start defending yourself, argument and reactive escalation are imminent. Be prepared to end the conversation immediately and if that fails, perhaps because your partner follows you, trying to provoke you, leave the room or even the house, as described earlier. You will need to identify your own infection point. This is not the right time to vent your feelings. Instead, exit from the interaction, calm down, rethink your own mistakes, replan, and then try to offer your opinion again. Strive to adhere to every word you planned and utter not one syllable more. In this way, you will progress ever closer toward being able to state your views without defending them, regardless of how hard and how often they are attacked.

After the interaction, it is essential that you learn to not react to your partner's retributions or attempted provocations, no matter what form they take or how long they continue. They may last for days, weeks, or months and include such common reactions as pouting, laying blame, raving, criticizing, getting drunk, working late, and verbally attacking the children and your family. Include this in your plan, too, for without this anticipation you will invariably get sucked back in. Rehearse every part of it, over and over. Plan it in your head, practice it with a friend, write it down on paper. Do whatever it takes to make your plan as concrete and well prepared as possible. Always aim to just state your view, rather than trying to promote it or apologize for it. Keep in mind that yours is only one person's opinion and also that you are not helping to decide someone's fate at a murder trial—although sometimes it may seem like it!

Note: Do not interpret this to suggest that you should accept or live in an abusive situation while waiting for your spouse to get over his anger. If there are any hints that your situation could become physically dangerous or damaging, you will have to try to work through your problems while living separately, and with professional help.

## First Failure, Then Success

Few people succeed in their first few attempts, and most fail many times as they go through the stages of planning their changes: forgetting them when an encounter begins but remembering them afterward; remembering the planned changes during the encounter but feeling unable to initiate them; and finally putting them into effect. The key to your success will be to keep pushing yourself to learn and improve on your approach, using each failure to discover a little more about yourself and to gain self-determination along with self-control. After a reactive encounter always trace back the sequence of events that led to it rather than simply giving up. These distressing interactions will repeat themselves many times at first, so use them to your advantage.

Always keep in mind that your goal is to express and respect your mutual differentness. And remember that your partner's reaction is normal and unavoidable but will also be temporary, even though at first it will be intense, persistent, and apparently endless. Your partner is not purposely being "mean," although it may appear that way, but is reacting with typical old brain behavior. Keep in mind that at first the difficult burden of change is on one partner, and that the other will resist and attempt to undo that change at the beginning. But also remember that if one person does not take the initiative, the relationship will never improve.

Resolve to concentrate on preventing or extricating yourself from each reactive encounter, rather than on the reasons for your partner's behavior. Though it is true that all of us have quirks left over from childhood, the things we can deal with are in the present. Though this will take a good deal of effort over a considerable period of time, it cannot be bypassed. Failure to make this effort will mean continuation of your problems, in spite of all your hopes to the contrary. Until you have overcome your own inner opposition and your reactions to your partner's, you will not be able to communicate your true opinion, and nothing of value will have been accomplished. The bottom line is to learn to state your position without being drawn into an argument, rather than letting it remain a source of conflict until you divorce or die. Once you have succeeded in expressing one difference of opinion, you will be able to take on another and will find that this gets easier with each one. The more you can use your reactive encounters to identify your triggers and then work at correcting them, the better your life and relationship will become.

## First Signs of Success

Learning how to defuse an argument will go a long way toward relieving the conflicts between you and your partner. The first sign that you are succeeding will be a mutual cessation of attack or retaliation when differences between you emerge. Someone described the stage in this way: "I can now state what I feel and not get attacked for it. But I still have a difficult time believing it will last." After this comes the stage where each of you will be more open to the differences between you. This has been described thus: "After years of uncomfortable silence, unspoken thoughts, and conflicting but unvoiced opinions, we've started talking again. I'm actually rediscovering the person I married and starting to like him again."

Eventually, over a longer period, a mutual respect for your differences will develop. One man expressed this very well in his description of his partner: "For years I thought she was kind of 'ditzy.' I still don't understand how she arrives at her conclusions, but I have learned to pay attention to them. She's frequently right both about people and situations." And a woman said about her husband: "I started off attacking his beliefs and views, then I learned to appreciate them. Now they're a source of stimulation to me."

## FORCED AGREEMENT WORKSHEETS

*You may wish to make several photocopies of the following pages while they are still blank, since you may be repeating these exercises several times.*

The following worksheets are designed to help you identify, design, and implement a plan that will eliminate forced agreement between you and your partner. After reading chapter 5, you will have some idea of what you would like to change about this issue in your relationship. Describe that goal here. (For example, "My goal is to get to the point where my partner and I can discuss our differences without attacking or giving in to the other.")

_____

_____

_____

The exercises that follow are not meant to be completed in one sitting. As you discover more about yourself, go back and fill in any blanks, or perhaps modify some you have already filled in. As you know, self-analysis cannot be accomplished all at once, but it will be very productive to use your ongoing reactive encounters as opportunities to add to your self-knowledge. So remember, don't lose heart if you find you are leaving empty spaces.

## OBSERVING YOUR DISAGREEMENTS

Reading over chapter 5 from Observing Your Disagreements (page 90) on will be helpful for the exercises that follow.

1. As before, it will be easier to identify this issue in your own relationship if you can first observe it in others. Describe below how you have seen forced agreement in at least one other relationship. Include who/what triggered it, what followed, and the effects on all parties. (For example, "When I visited my neighbors, the wife expressed an opinion on how to barbecue some shrimp. Her husband first attacked her method, then verbally attacked her. This caused a lot of tension among everyone for the rest of the evening.")

_____

_____

_____

## OBSERVING YOUR PARTNER FORCING AGREEMENT

Because in many relationships forced agreement is so subtle, the following exercises are designed to help you identify this issue more clearly. In this section, you will identify it in your partner. In the next section, you will identify it in yourself.

1. After your next argument, check off which position(s) your partner took.

Rightness ☐   Truth ☐
Winning ☐

Describe how this usually occurs. (For example, "I noticed he has to be in the right whenever I express a different opinion on money matters.")

_____

_____

_____

2. Many people use (or imply) "we" to express their individual view, as if it were the only view possible. Does your partner use "we" when expressing a personal view?

Yes   ☐            No   ☐

3. If you checked yes, describe how. (For example, "Whenever the topic of a vacation comes up, she presents where she wants to go as if we both want to go there, when in fact I don't.")

_____

_____

_____

4. This exercise is designed to help you discern what your partner truly believes on a particular topic (a true "I" position) in comparison to the one expressed in the old brain reaction to you (a reactive "I" position).

     Below describe what you think was your partner's true position and reactive position. What was the motivation for the reaction?

| Partner's True "I" | Partner's Reactive "I" | Partner's Motivation |
|---|---|---|
| (For example, "Wanted to paint the living room blue.") | (For example, "Because I wanted blue also, he switched to mauve.") | (For example, "Spite.") |

_____

5. Check off what happened when you disagreed with your partner's view.

Ignored me                  ☐     Ignored the topic         ☐

Gave in to keep the peace ☐     Attacked me verbally    ☐

Retaliated                 ☐     Attacked my view      ☐

Manipulated/pressured          Tried to make me feel

   me to change my view ☐       wrong/guilty         ☐

Other(s)

_____

_____

6. Explain those you checked off. (For example, "My girlfriend refused to visit my family after I disagreed with her over whether the view out of our living room window was beautiful.")

_____

_____

_____

7. Describe how this affected both you and your relationship. (For example, "It made me resentful and afraid to express my view.")

_____

_____

_____

8. How long did these effects last?
Hours ☐     Days ☐     Weeks ☐     Months ☐

9. This exercise is designed to highlight the contradiction between your partner's words and actions. Does your partner claim to be open to your views, but undermines them when you express yourself?
Yes                    ☐          No                        ☐

   If your answer was yes, observe your partner's actions rather than his or her words. (When you see those actions change, you will know that significant change is occurring in your partner.)

_____

_____

_____

10. In your last argument, did your partner attack or ignore your view?
Attacked it              ☐          Ignored it              ☐

11. If your partner attacked your view, describe the point where you couldn't stop yourself from defending your view. (For example, "After the third time I explained my view, I lost control and couldn't stop myself from defending it.")

_____

_____

12. This was your point of reactive infection. As you probably noticed, all communication past this point was counterproductive and hurt rather than helped your interaction. Describe the escalation that occurred after this point. (For example, "I called him names and he retaliated with more names.")

_____

_____

_____

If you left any blanks in the above exercises, use your future reactive encounters as learning aids and fill in the blanks later. Don't get disheartened if you couldn't fill in any of the above; just keep looking at your future reactive encounters—they will give you more than enough opportunities for filling in the blanks.

## OBSERVING YOUR OWN FORCED AGREEMENTS

Now that you have a clearer view of your partner, use the following exercises to uncover your own attempts to stifle differentness in your relationship.

I. Which position(s) do you most frequently take in a disagreement with your partner?
I am right    ☐        I am telling the truth    ☐        I want to win    ☐
Enter the dates you took this position.

_____

_____

_____

2. Describe when they occur. (For example, "I notice it's important for me to be in the right and win when it concerns the children, my job, and what we eat for dinner.")

_____

_____

_____

3. Describe the areas where you use (or imply) the word "we" when it is accurate only to say "I." (For example, "Whenever the discussion of which supermarket has the best prices comes up, I express as our view what is my own view. In actuality, my boyfriend doesn't share my view.")

_____

_____

_____

4. To determine which of the opinions you express are merely in reaction to your partner rather than those you truly hold, fill in the table below.

| My True "I" | My Reactive "I" | My Motivation |
|---|---|---|
| (For example, "I wanted to see a romance.") | (For example, "I agreed to see a murder movie.") | (For example, "I placated him.") |

5. Your own true "I" positions can be difficult to discern if you are not used to doing so. However, this can be learned. If you are having a difficult time figuring out what your views really are, write down the name or names of people you think can help you sort out your true versus your reactive position. (For example, "I will talk to my friend Joan and my brother.")

_____

_____

_____

6. Even though you may find it difficult to look at what you do to your partner, it is important to push yourself to do this. As you know, the key to resolving this issue lies more in confronting yourself than in trying to change your partner.

When your partner disagrees with you, write down how it feels. (For example, "I felt hurt when he said he didn't like the meal I had praised.")

_____

_____

_____

7. Record what you did next.

Ignored my partner ☐                    Ignored the topic ☐
Gave in to keep the peace ☐            Attacked my partner's view ☐
Attacked my partner                     Retaliated ☐
  verbally ☐                            Manipulated/pressured my
Tried to make my partner                  partner to change views ☐
  feel wrong/guilty ☐
Other(s)

_____

8. Describe how your lack of tolerance of your partner's differentness affects both you personally and your relationship. (For example, "It left me very upset for hours, and it ruined our week together.")

_____

_____

9. Do you say you want to know your partner's opinion, but attack it when it is given?

Yes ☐                                   No ☐

10. If you checked yes, describe how this occurs. (For example, "Whenever I ask for her view and it differs from mine, I make fun of it.")

_____

_____

## ACCEPTING YOUR PARTNER'S DIFFERENTNESS

Now that you have identified your partner's differentness, the following exercises will help you begin to accept them.

1. Pick an issue where you attack your partner's differentness and write it down here.

_____

_____

2. Describe how you attacked your partner. (For example, "I told him he was foolish.")

_____

_____

_____

3. Now write down exactly what you will do differently next time. (For example, "I will keep myself from calling him foolish.")

_____

_____

_____

4. Because you are changing a habitual response, it is quite normal to experience an inner struggle between wanting and not wanting to change it. Describe that struggle here. (For example, "Part of me knows I need to not attack her view, but another part tells me I will be walked on if I don't express what I feel.")

_____

_____

_____

5. Though it is *imperative* that you do not vent your negative feelings to your partner about the differentness, it is equally important to release your feelings in some other way. Make a list of some physical ways you can safely express and release your anger. (For example, "I will exercise, go dancing.")

_____

_____

_____

6. In my experience, immediate successes in the above exercises are very rare—perhaps a rate of five percent. Most people go through a number of stages and failed attempts before being successful. This exercise will help to reassure you about your failures. You have already gone through the first stage of planning your change.

The second stage: Check off the times you remembered your planned new response only *after* your reactive interaction occurred.

| | | | |
|---|---|---|---|
| 1st missed opportunity | ☐ | 6th missed opportunity | ☐ |
| 2nd missed opportunity | ☐ | 7th missed opportunity | ☐ |
| 3rd missed opportunity | ☐ | 8th missed opportunity | ☐ |
| 4th missed opportunity | ☐ | 9th missed opportunity | ☐ |
| 5th missed opportunity | ☐ | 10th missed opportunity | ☐ |

Note: Don't look at these tries as failures, but as a step at a time closer to success.

The third stage is being aware to not react in your usual way during an encounter, while still being unable to change it. Check off below each of your unsuccessful efforts.

| | | | |
|---|---|---|---|
| 1st missed opportunity | ☐ | 6th missed opportunity | ☐ |
| 2nd missed opportunity | ☐ | 7th missed opportunity | ☐ |
| 3rd missed opportunity | ☐ | 8th missed opportunity | ☐ |
| 4th missed opportunity | ☐ | 9th missed opportunity | ☐ |
| 5th missed opportunity | ☐ | 10th missed opportunity | ☐ |

The fourth stage: Here you have made a successful change, so congratulations!

You have just eliminated a recurring problem in your relationship and life. After celebrating your well-earned victory, start again. Pick another area or topic in which you have not accepted your partner's differentness, and then fill in more blank worksheets, similar to those you just completed. In this way you will decrease and eventually eliminate the areas in which you have not been able to accept your partner's differentness. The more you can eliminate, the greater the impact will be on your relationship.

The above work can be done before, or at the same time as, the following set of exercises—whichever you're most comfortable with. Keep in mind that it will become easier with each new attempt. The first one is always the most difficult.

## GETTING YOUR PARTNER TO ACCEPT YOUR DIFFERENTNESS

Now you will turn your efforts to learning how to get your partner to accept your differentness. Whoever is on the receiving (as opposed to the initiating) end of a new behavior will tend to escalate their reaction to that behavior as they try to maintain the familiar status quo. The next set of exercises is designed to address this problem.

1. Pick one of your opinions that your partner has attacked. Describe it here. (For example, "Whenever I say I'd like to see a musical and go to a Chinese restaurant afterward, he convinces me to see a comedy and go to an Italian restaurant.")

_____

_____

_____

2. Now that you know your position, express it in the form of an opinion or preference. Write down specifically what you will say. (For example, "When this issue comes up again, I will say, 'I'd prefer to see a musical and eat Chinese food.' Or I will say, 'It's my opinion/my view . . .' Or 'I believe/ feel/think . . .'")

_____

_____

_____

3. Anticipating your partner's reactions in the following exercises will be very beneficial. First, try writing down these anticipated responses in pencil, and then go back to change them if they turn out otherwise.

Once you have expressed your different view, your partner will try to get you to drop or change it. Below is a list of ways people do this. Check off the ways you think *your* partner will use. Afterward, go back and check off the actual reactions if they were different from the ones you would have expected.

My partner will:

| | | | |
|---|---|---|---|
| Ignore me/ignore my view ☐ | | Attack my view | ☐ |
| Accuse/attack me ☐ | | Retaliate | ☐ |
| Manipulate/pressure me | | Try to make me feel | |
|   to change my view ☐ | |   guilty/wrong | ☐ |
| Other(s) | | | |

_____

_____

4. Your partner will try first to draw you into defending your view and eventually into dropping it. If this succeeds, don't worry about it. It is rare that this does *not* happen initially.

Below is a list of the ways most people defend their views. Check off which ones you used.

| | | | |
|---|---|---|---|
| I repeatedly explained my view. | ☐ | I tried to reason with my partner. | ☐ |
| I answered my partner's charges. | ☐ | I justified my position. | ☐ |
| I sought my partner's permission to say "my piece." | ☐ | I sought my partner's approval. | ☐ |
| | | I attacked my partner. | ☐ |
| | | I attacked my partner's view. | ☐ |

5. Describe here exactly how you will refrain from defending your view in the future and how you will express this to your partner. (For example, "When my partner attacks my view, instead of justifying it, I will say I have nothing further to say about it.")

When attacked, I will keep from defending my view by:

_____

_____

_____

6. If your partner continues attacking (which is highly likely), you will need to break off contact as discussed in chapter 3. Describe here how you think your partner will try to prevent you from breaking off the reactive contact. (For example, "She will follow me into the basement and shout through the closed door.")

_____

_____

_____

7. After a short-term escalation, there is a strong probability that your partner will retaliate over the long term. Describe how you think this will occur. (For example, "Will get drunk. Work late. Ridicule the children. Poke fun at my views around friends.")

_____

_____

_____

8. How long do you think this will last?

Hours ☐      Days ☐      Weeks ☐      Months ☐

Don't be discouraged if you find you are confused during your interactions with him. This is a sign that reactive infection has occurred. The solution is to back out and try again.

Following is a list of Do's and Don'ts that you may want to refer to occasionally.

| Do | Don't |
|---|---|
| State your own view. | Try to "sell" your view or justify it. |
| Keep your perspective. | Lose hope. (Failures are to be |
| Vent your feelings to a trusted friend. | expected.) |
| | Vent your feelings to your partner. |
| Disengage as soon as you become reactive. | Regard your partner's behavior as unique. |
| Try to learn from your failed efforts. | Give up. |
| Stick to your plan. | |
| Try to anticipate your partner's reactions. | |
| Rehearse your planned changes. | |

9. Just as with your struggles to accept your partner's differentness, getting your partner to accept your differentness is rarely successful right away. Below are the stages you will most likely go through. You have already passed the stage of planning your change.

In the second stage, you will probably have forgotten your planned change. Either you didn't express your true opinion or, more likely, you defended yourself against your partner's attacks. Check off your unsuccessful attempts.

| | | | |
|---|---|---|---|
| 1st missed opportunity | ☐ | 6th missed opportunity | ☐ |
| 2nd missed opportunity | ☐ | 7th missed opportunity | ☐ |
| 3rd missed opportunity | ☐ | 8th missed opportunity | ☐ |
| 4th missed opportunity | ☐ | 9th missed opportunity | ☐ |
| 5th missed opportunity | ☐ | 10th missed opportunity | ☐ |

In the third stage, you are likely to be aware of what you are doing wrong during the reactive interaction, but are still unable to change it. Check off these efforts.

| | | | |
|---|---|---|---|
| 1st missed opportunity | ☐ | 6th missed opportunity | ☐ |
| 2nd missed opportunity | ☐ | 7th missed opportunity | ☐ |
| 3rd missed opportunity | ☐ | 8th missed opportunity | ☐ |
| 4th missed opportunity | ☐ | 9th missed opportunity | ☐ |
| 5th missed opportunity | ☐ | 10th missed opportunity | ☐ |

You have reached the fourth stage when you make your change successfully. Good for you! After savoring your victory, go back and try to do the same thing for another topic or area. The more areas you can do this in, the more problems you will have eliminated.

# CHAPTER 6

# Dealing with "Who is to Blame"

The dictionary defines fault as "a failure to do what is right," and blame as "to attribute responsibility to." But for our purposes here, the difference between the two is irrelevant, and they will be treated as the same. Issues of who is to blame and who is responsible are common sources of relationship trouble, as illustrated by the following remarks:

> I could be fifty miles away and if something goes wrong in her life, it's my fault!

> Whenever I point out a mistake he's made, he immediately attacks me and we get into an argument.

> No matter what problem I try to discuss with her, when the conversation's over, I always feel like I'm to blame, even though I know I'm not.

If you find you are experiencing a similar situation in your relationship, the issue you are struggling with is the one of responsibility, or who is "at fault." For couples in distress, this issue is a tripwire to disagreement and emotional turmoil. The question of who "needs to get help" is also often raised, with each trying to get the other to admit to having a "problem" and needing help. Some times this struggle is in the open and clear, but just as often it is covert and ambiguous. In some couples neither person is willing to accept responsibility, and in others one unwillingly assumes the blame for both in order to keep the peace. This struggle over the issue of responsibility contributes greatly to the emotional reactivity, communication breakdown, and loss of caring between partners. As one young woman said, "Whenever either of us gets on the subject of who's at fault, so many charges are thrown back and forth, we forget what we wanted to say. Instead, all we do is attack one another."

Many partners continue to battle about these issues without progress or resolution. And, as with all reactive behavior, the issue of fault grows progressively larger, consuming more of their relationship and personal lives over the years. As a major source of the reactivity in relationships, it gives rise to considerable turmoil and feelings of confusion. Each partner becomes more and more baffled about what to believe or how much to trust even his own thoughts. As one man reported, "After talking with her, I'm so confused I don't know what to believe or what I need to change. I know I can't be at fault for everything, but just what I'm responsible for I have no idea, since she blames me for everything." Such confusion always leads to the kind of profound self-doubt that was expressed in this comment: "I know what I want to say until I talk to him about it. Then he convinces me that what I'm talking about doesn't exist. Or does it? I'm always questioning myself and wondering how much I'm imagining or whether I'm losing my mind!"

## Fault as a Trigger to Reactivity

As discussed earlier, when an emotional trigger is tripped, our old brain switches on and we immediately become irrational and combative. Cooperation ceases, making reasonable discussion and problem-solving impossible. Issues of fault and blame are especially potent triggers since they mobilize our fears about having to change, our pride about being right, and are often raised in ways that provoke a reaction. The most difficult thing for us humans to say is, "I am wrong and need to change." Statements that attribute fault are usually made to get someone to admit an error. However, your partner will resist seeing any errors and will block communications that imply fault: the need to maintain self-deception and the status quo takes over. To understand this better, think about how difficult it has always been for you to look at your own errors.

In addition, blame is most frequently communicated in the form of "you" statements such as, "What is wrong with you?" and "Why did you (or didn't you)?" and so on. Such things are said when we are upset and our old brain is looking for a fight. These statements can be laced with sarcasm, cuts, and covert insults, and may be delivered in a belligerent tone of voice. One husband recounted, "When she uses that tone, it goes right through me. I may agree with what she says, but the tone in which it's said makes me so mad I wouldn't admit to being at fault if my life depended on it." Frequently such statements suggest that the other partner had ulterior motives or that something injurious was done intentionally and may even have been enjoyed. Whether or not such motives were involved, saying so accomplishes nothing constructive and creates a destructive atmosphere. In most "you" statements, provocative words are used (for example, "immature," "sick," "mean") and contentious past events are referred to ("the time you lied to me three years ago"). And, as with all old brain reactions, loss of control means it is rare that only one "you" statement is made.

Often, many or all of these aspects are combined in a remark like this one, said in an angry and biting way: "You're ruining our marriage, and you're too stupid to even see it! What's wrong with you?" If you were on the receiving end of such a verbal attack, even if you believed that it was true, would you listen and admit to it? Would you be able to respond with reason and cooperation? Or would you defend, deny, justify, excuse, and counterattack, just to preserve what little dignity you felt you had left?

By their very nature, "you" statements provoke and escalate issues of fault and responsibility to a point where cooperative discussion and resolution become impossible.

## Stating Your Position without Blaming

If the issue of fault has been a problem in your relationship, it does not have to remain one. The rest of this chapter and the worksheets at the end deal with how to discuss your position without provoking an argument. You will learn how to say what you want to say without attacking your partner, as well as how to keep from getting flustered and deflected by accusations, evasions, and blaming.

Remember that laying blame will always cause a reaction. Until conscious plans and determined efforts are used to halt it, no couple can escape its influence. You might ask, "What can I say and do to get my partner to stop blaming me for everything that goes wrong?" In fact, it is what you *do not* say and do that will stop it. A mistake we often make is to react to attacks by defending, justifying, offering repeated explanations, pleading for understanding, seeking approval or permission for what we want to say, and placating our partners to "keep them quiet." Most of this occurs with the partner in the heat of battle and in an old brain state. These responses always fail because *any* engagement will fuel reactivity. But once you learn how to talk to your partner without placing blame *or* defending yourself against blame, you will eliminate this fuel. One husband described it this way: "When I learned how to respond to my wife's accusations without defending myself, her finger-pointing ended, and after twenty-five years we finally put this behind us."

Underlying this discussion is the assumption that each of us is responsible for our own actions. It is one thing to believe this, but in practice, particularly during times of stress, it can be very difficult to act on. Instead, when we are upset and in an old brain state, it is both easy and human to lay blame and place the fault on others. Thus, one partner will say to the other, "You're making me angry and upset." But one person is never solely responsible for the problems a couple experiences, no matter how it appears. As we have seen, one partner can begin to resolve a relationship's problems by changing certain behaviors, rather than continuing to blame the partner. And when this is done, the entire situation will improve.

Blaming can take many forms. One of the most common is blaming one's parents for the way one behaves instead of doing something about the behavior—using one's difficult past as an excuse to avoid change. Another is blaming the opposite sex for the predicament one repeatedly finds oneself in. Thus, many men point to how women are at fault, while many women see themselves as victims of men. Whether or not any of these things are true, once we are faced with a problem behavior or situation, it becomes *our own* responsibility to do something about it or our problems will continue. The point is that there is always a flip side to relationship problems, and this is the side for which we can take responsibility. In most cases, the submissive woman who is "walked on" by her domineering and controlling partner can either point to his domineering ways or look at her own dependent and submissive behavior as contributing to her misery and victimization. She can then do something about *her* behavior. The husband of a "spendaholic" wife can either blame her for the unhappiness she "causes" him or see himself as allowing her spending patterns to control his life and look for ways to end that control. The woman who feels she is living with a "baby" can either identify his immature behavior as the source of her sadness or see her own babying ways as contributing to it, and then do something about them. (See chapter 8 on pursuit and distance for further discussion of this issue.)

Whether you see yourself as victim or participant is really more a matter of which side of the coin you choose to focus on: your mate's problems or your own. And the side you pick will be the deciding factor between continuing or ending your relationship problems. Trying to force your partner to see his or her faults will only worsen the relationship. The confusion, turmoil, and arguments that follow this attempt are all the result of reactive overload. We know that such a direct approach is bound to be unsuccessful and that this kind of problem must be approached indirectly. As a marriage counselor, I have seen that when we focus on ourselves and work with our own problems, our life with our partner improves, and if we do not, our life as a couple continues to deteriorate.

## Venting Your Feelings to Your Partner

People often believe that there is nothing wrong with venting, or expressing to your partner what you feel about him or her whenever you feel it. But in a relationship that is undergoing problems, indiscriminately releasing or venting what you think and feel will only make your situation worse. A troubled relationship cannot absorb the expression of still more negative feelings because it is already overwhelmed by them. And further spontaneous expressions of hostility, frustration, and resentment will only serve to drive a couple further apart. For this reason, I do not recommend venting your feelings to your partner, particularly when you are upset. While you may initially feel better because you expressed what you "really" thought, after this moment has passed, your situation will further deteriorate, as both you and your partner will be unable to forgive or forget what was said or how it was said. And you in turn, will feel even worse.

If improving your relationship is your first priority, then remember that it will be counterproductive to vent your feelings whenever there is tension between you. You can, however, safely release your feelings with a friend, or you may choose to go for a drive and scream it out alone. Later, when you are calmer, you will better be able to guide a conversation past argument and toward discussion, carefully choosing what you say and how you say it. Your partner will not be able to see his contributions to your problems until they are presented in a way that he can accept. As long as they are presented reactively, this will not happen.

In this chapter, you will learn to talk about issues with a minimum of accusation and argument. Often, this alone will help untangle a conflict and move a relationship past a deadlock. At other times, even though a problem issue is calmly discussed, the behavior remains unchanged. The chapters following this one will help you deal with such an outcome.

### Planning for Successful Communication about Problems

The most difficult part of communicating contentious feelings and opinions is learning to not react to your partner's retaliations, no matter how provocative and malicious they seem to be. Having a plan is essential for accomplishing this. Again, the approach will be to observe, plan, and make your attempts, most likely failing in the beginning, then replanning and trying again until you succeed.

## *Making Observations*

The worksheets at the end of this chapter will show you how to dissect future reactive encounters with your partner and how to identify their source. Again, you will find it easier to begin by observing other people, then your partner, and finally, yourself. To discover what happens with fault-finding can sometimes be easy, but at other times it is more difficult. You will learn to anticipate when and how your partner blames you, noting how often and around what issues fault and blame are used. You will also observe what you do and how you seem to make your partner angry and blaming. You will learn to observe your partner's use of "you" statements, noting whether there is a discrepancy between what is said and what is done, particularly under stress. Whenever there is such a discrepancy, it is best to ignore the *words* while still holding your partner accountable for the *actions*. Actions reveal where our beliefs really lie.

In your future reactive exchanges, you will observe how your partner deals with remarks of yours that sound like blaming. Some people simply block the exchange. As one man described it, "She'll change the subject without answering me." Others will try to confuse. A woman described this vividly: "He twists what I say into pretzels." Others may just evade the issue. You will try to identify how your partner counterattacks, if there is a particular pattern, and around which subjects this occurs. You will learn to notice how you react to these counterattacks. Some people try to defend themselves by justifying or explaining their remarks. Others may plead for approval. You may be able to identify a point when you find it impossible to stop reacting to your partner's accusations. It will be very helpful to isolate this point of reactive infection. You will be able to make note of the turmoil that occurs within you and between the two of you after this point. Once you have done all this, you will be able to use what you learn about your partner to identify your own contribution to your encounters.

## *Talking To Your Partner Without Blaming*

To convey your message without blaming, you must think clearly about the point you want to get across *before* you speak. Afterward will be too late. Below are some examples of what can happen in the absence of such clarity. A woman had been in a relationship with a man for eight years. Whenever she spoke to him about divorcing his estranged wife and making a commitment to her, she did so sarcastically because she was so upset over this issue. Afterward she said, "These discussions always lead to confusion, anger, and turmoil for me, and a bad argument with him. I'm so upset, I don't sleep for days." Another woman described her situation in this way: "My husband had an affair and says it's over. He wants me to trust him again. However, his continued contact with and calls from the woman make me question whether the affair is really over. I can't talk to him about it without losing my temper, and then I talk to him in a very ugly way. That always starts a screaming match." And a husband reported wanting to discuss a problem with his father-in-law, contrary to his wife's wishes: "Every time I say I'm going to talk to him about it, I blame my wife for the problems her father has caused us. This always leads to a scene."

### Clearly Stating Your "I" Position

In order to make your point without reactivity, state only your true "I" position. Be very clear about your point or message, rather than focusing on getting a reaction from your partner. Put all your efforts into saying exactly what you mean without being critical or vindictive. If you are unused to thinking along this line, ask yourself, "What is the message I want to get across, as opposed to what I want to say in reaction to my partner?" While the difference between the two appears subtle, it is crucial for successful communication. For the woman whose boyfriend of eight years would not make a commitment, her true "I" position was expressed as, "I want to find out exactly when he is going to commit to me, if ever." And for the woman who was unsure whether her husband's affair was over, her true "I" position was, "I want proof it is over before I begin to trust him again. Part of that proof will be no more calls and contact with her. Until that time, I can't trust him." And for the man who wanted to talk to his father-in-law, though his wife objected, his "I" position was, "I need to talk to him about it, whether or not you approve. It is between him and me." (What you can do if these problems continue, even though you *have* unprovocatively stated your position, will be discussed in the following chapters.)

Once you are clear in your mind about the point you want to make, your next task will be to plan for conveying your position in a nonreactive way. It is likely that everything you say will at first be perceived as an attempt to provoke. (How to handle this will be discussed shortly.) But your first step will be to say what you want to say unprovocatively. And the best way to accomplish this is by not making "you" statements, because whenever you initiate a discussion with a "you", you will start an argument. And if in an argument you respond with one, you will surely continue the argument. So always keep to "I" statements, making them as brief and to the point as possible.

This example helps to illustrate this point: A woman decided to get her own checking account because her husband's impulse buying was draining both her and their earnings. She knew he would try to challenge her if she brought up his spending, and that it would end in an argument. So she stated her "I" position as clearly and as unprovocatively as possible by saying, "I decided to get my own checking account to simplify my finances." She made no further statements or explanations. She did not speak sarcastically, loudly, or bitingly. She did not lecture or rub it in (although there was good reason to). She did not defend her statement, nor did she present it in a permission-seeking way. She did not justify it or speak in an accusatory or defiant manner. (Although, of course, it could still be perceived to be any or all of these.) She also avoided using such trigger words as "spendthrift." There was no mention of who "started it," whose "fault" it was, or what was "wrong" with him. Nor did she imply any motives for her partner's behavior or try to "shape him up." She stated her "I" position and absolutely nothing more, simply conveying her intention to act in her own best interest.

The following examples of typical "you" statements are followed by clearly defined alternative "I" statements:

A woman who was upset at her partner's constantly analyzing her burst out, "I'm tired of you analyzing me. You're the one who needs analysis!" Another way would be to say calmly, "As I've said before, I don't want to be analyzed, and I will not listen any more."

Another woman, confronting her husband about his poor treatment of her, announced, "I am your partner and not some subservient creature! You will not treat me that way from now on!" A less reactive way to convey the same thing would have been to say, "I'm your partner, and I won't be treated otherwise any longer."

A husband, disturbed by his wife's immature behavior when they are out together, told her, "I don't go out with you because you act like an ass in public. You're forty-five, not fifteen, so act like it!" A less volatile way to convey the same message might be to say, "I don't go out with you because I don't want to be embarrassed any longer." (Sometimes the word "you" cannot be avoided, but its use can be minimized.)

A woman who was tired of working at her job plus being responsible for all of the household duties told her partner, "From now on you'll be washing your own clothes! I'm too tired to clean up after you." A less provocative approach might have been to say, "I'm too overworked, and will only be cleaning my own clothes from now on." (This exactly expresses her "I" position.)

A man who was trying to discuss the issue of not being heard by his wife declared, "You don't want to hear my side!" Along with using "you," he is implying a negative motive on her part, though perhaps she does want to hear his side. Even if she doesn't, pointing it out is not likely to help matters. Instead, he might have said, "I don't feel listened to when I have something to say on the subject of . . ."

A woman who was dealing with her husband's drinking declared, "You're drinking again after you promised you wouldn't. You're a hopeless case! That's the reason I'm going to move out." A less reactive way to communicate the same things, without adding even more stress to an already volatile situation, could be to say simply, "I'm moving out. Things have not worked out here, as I've said before. And I won't live, as I have said before, with alcohol as a part of my marriage." The second way of speaking leaves out any pleading, blame, apology, embellishment, judgment, or criticism. Though her husband would most likely react strongly to whatever she said, in this way she could at least minimize her own contribution to his reaction.

All such statements, if made firmly and with conviction, will let your partner know just how strongly you feel about an issue. But keep in mind that these are not magic words that will cause your partner to change on the spot. Rather, they offer a way of conveying something important, without reactivity, and bringing you both a step closer to resolution of a contentious issue. It is important to stay away from making statements about what your partner is "doing to" you. Instead, concentrate on what you have been allowing to be done to you, and take responsibility for change where it can have some positive outcome. If you were to say, "You're making me angry," this would place the responsibility for your anger entirely onto your partner. It would also convey that you believe your partner has the power to *make* you angry. To be sure, your partner can "push your trigger buttons," insult you, and hurt your feelings, but you are still the one to decide whether or not to retaliate in anger. You might say instead, "I am angered by what you're doing," taking responsibility for the anger. It also points to a specific behavior rather than a condemnation of your partner in general. This is not to deny that you are furious, but rather to do something constructive with your anger. (See the following chapters for much more about anger.)

If you nevertheless feel you must blame your partner, you can include something about your own contribution for a more balanced statement. Thus, for every comment that places responsibility on your partner, include one about your own share. Below are some typical examples of such balanced statements.

I'm tired of your 'poor me' routine, but I'm just as tired with myself falling for it.

I think you're very domineering (or manipulative, controlling, uncaring), but I think I'm too submissive (or easy to manipulate or to control, or dependent on your caring).

You chewed me out again, but I let myself be chewed out.

You're so impulsive, but at times I am too.

Once you have identified your share of responsibility, you can do something about it. Don't forget that change is always initiated by the one who is the most uncomfortable in the relationship. In the above examples, this would be the one who is submissive, or being "chewed out." When you make this change, your partner will come closer to changing too. Since this form of expression will be new to you, it is especially necessary to plan and even to privately rehearse what you want to say, in order for it to come out right when the time comes. (See the worksheets at the end of this chapter.)

## Dealing with Both Your Inner and Your Partner's Opposition

During this process you are bound to experience an inner struggle between the forces against and for change. Anti-change forces will pressure you to vent your feelings as you always have, by making "you" statements, critically pointing out your partner's faults and irresponsibilities, saying things in a sarcastic or biting tone, reproaching your partner about past behavior and pointing out your "right" to do so. Restraining this impulse will at first leave you feeling confused and unable to think of an unprovocative way to communicate. Also, new ways of speaking will feel awkward, and you will be afraid of hurting your partner. As one man described, "If I say what I really think, rather than saying what I think she wants to hear, I'm afraid I'll hurt her." But there is no way to avoid this pain, as change always involves pain. We either deal with it once and for all or we drag the pain out indefinitely. Be prepared that part of you also will resist admitting to yourself, and especially to your partner, that you, too, have been at fault.

Before you can successfully express yourself in this selective and restrained fashion, you will have to move through the learning stages described in previous chapters. People often fail during this time because they try to force the issue of fault and responsibility down their partner's throat by lecturing, pleading, or manipulating. Such efforts will make your partner even less cooperative. When you catch yourself doing this (because everyone does, at some point), work toward stating your "I" position nonreactively.

While what has been described here will not actually resolve your problem, this is where the real work of handling your partner's attempts to move back toward argument and finger-pointing must begin. That change is always met with opposition is a fact of life, like death and taxes. So when you first state your true "I" position, your partner will vigorously oppose it. One woman described this concisely: "Whenever I state where I really stand, my boyfriend relentlessly attacks it, and I end up getting drawn into an argument." On the other hand, it may be your partner who initiates a discussion and blames you. But in each instance, you must learn to identify the area in which your partner blames you and to observe exactly what is said and how it is said. When your partner tries to blame you for a problem, use your new brain to think for a moment while you are still calm. Try to understand what part is truly your own responsibility. Then try to distinguish between what you know you are responsible for and what your partner is trying to blame you for. You will have to steer through accusations, evasions, and denial without becoming sidetracked by them. And to accomplish this, you have to be very clear in your own mind about what it is you want to convey.

The woman whose boyfriend of eight years would not make a commitment to her found that whenever she brought up divorcing his estranged wife, he twisted around what she said with evasions, denials, and exaggerations. For example, he might say, "It's not the way you see it. I'm committed to you. My wife is not number one in my life, you are." She reported that then, "I always go away thinking how unreasonable I've been, though I didn't think so before I talked to him."

The man with the father-in-law issue reported, "Every time I tell my wife I'm going to talk to my father-in-law about his intrusiveness, she attacks me, and I end up not doing it, hating her, and wondering if I'm really that unrealistic in what I want."

In order to get your message across without being sidetracked, do not defend, justify, plead, or explain your position more than twice. Never try to convince your partner to accept your view; never ridicule or attack your partner in reaction to a provocation. Never allow yourself to be lured or dragged down the road of whose fault it is, who started it, or who is right. Always remember to simply state your "I" position and concentrate on saying nothing more. For example, the woman with the alcoholic partner might say, "As I've stated before, I won't discuss anything with you while you have alcohol on your breath." To act in this way will take considerable advance thought, and must be planned ahead of time. Since such attacks will be repeated, you will have many opportunities to improve your response. For example, a woman whose jealous husband had accused her of sleeping with his friend learned to repeat her true "I" position, adding nothing more. She phrased it thus: "I didn't do anything, so I have nothing further to say on it." Before, she would have responded to his attack by explaining herself until she was enraged and exhausted.

And the husband who continued to have contact with his girlfriend after his wife had stated her position reacted by making excuses and twisting her words. Previously, she would respond by justifying herself and pleading for his cooperation, but now she only repeated her "I" position by saying, "I don't want her calling here any more!"

Your inner struggle will be between your old brain wanting the gratification of retaliation and your new brain trying to exert restraint. You will feel angry, confused, undecided, despairing, and hurt. You will probably also feel awkward and uncomfortable. And while struggling with all of these feelings, you will also have to deal with your partner's opposition. Once you have begun to communicate differently, your partner will be likely to react impulsively with increased accusations and blaming. When this happens, it is imperative that you say nothing in reaction. If you feel you must do something, let it be something constructive, such as physically removing yourself from the room. *Not* reacting to blame, no matter how intense, is what will ultimately reach your partner.

Many people fail at this point because they have not prepared themselves for this escalation of their partner's hostility; they expected their new form of communication to be immediately accepted. However, only when your partner's attacks fail to provoke a reaction in you will they end. Thus, it is very important to anticipate this. Perhaps you can imagine what form the attacks will take, whether they will become increasingly louder, or uglier, or more persistent. One woman described her partner's reaction to her nonengagement this way: "He doesn't directly attack me. He just gets very evasive, trying to talk me out of it." And one man reported his partner as saying, "I don't know what you want; you're asking too much." Whatever your own partner's response turns out to be, you must decide how to work it into your plan of remaining nonreactive.

It is very likely that you will go through all the stages discussed earlier: first identifying and planning your new form of communication, then losing your awareness of what you were going to do differently at the onset of a reactive engagement, then being able to remain aware but still not able to implement what you know, and finally, a successful follow-through.

To help yourself through these stages, watch for the physical signs of your own reactivity, for example, increased heart rate, tension in the pit of your stomach, perspiring or chilled hands, or raised voice. Also note what you say and how you say it, whether it is pleading for acceptance, justifying what you have said, explaining it more than twice, defending it, retaliating, or trying to persuade or gain approval. And prepare yourself to break off the discussion when any of these things happen and even to stop further contact if this becomes necessary. As with all reactive encounters, it is essential to disengage before you lose control. If you can see yourself about to lose control, you could say, "I don't want to discuss it any more right now. I'm getting too upset." Then go into another room or leave the house if need be. If you do not do this, reactive escalation will follow, together with an increasingly out-of-control argument. Remember that all communication will be counterproductive after reactive infection begins.

Once you have disengaged, you will need a way to release ten-

sion and clear your head. Aerobic exercise, such as walking or swim-
ming, is excellent, as is reading an engrossing book, becoming ab-
sorbed with a hobby, or talking things over with a sympathetic
friend—but never with your partner. Once your head is clearer, you
will be able to refocus on your own errors and plan your next effort.
Try again, and keep repeating these steps until you are successful.

If you experience confusion and personal turmoil, you will
know that you have been reactively "hooked." In this case, trace the
exchanges with your partner back to where the reactive symptoms
began and try again. Use your anger constructively to fuel your next
effort. One man did so by telling himself, "Damn it! The next time
she starts accusing me again, I won't allow myself to get pulled into
blaming her back. I'll stick to what I said I was going to do!" (While
it is true that if your partner had not "started" it, you would not be
having to do all this, on the other hand, if you had not continued reacting, you would also not be having to do this. Regardless of who
started it, the situation will continue until you stop your own participation.) So stay focused on the present, and keep away from pre-
occupation with your partner's or your own past (i.e. I'm so blaming because my parents are that way, or because my self-esteem is so
low.) Do not allow yourself to be drawn into an argument about
who "started it," whose "fault" it was, who did what to whom, or
why he (or you) act this way. All these lead inexorably to the death
of all caring. It will help to keep in mind that your partner's escalated provocative behavior will pass.

## Confronting Yourself

After you have successfully neither defended yourself nor attacked
your partner, your next step will be to consider the validity of what
your partner said. This painful task is necessary if your own problem behavior and the problems it spawns are to end. To accomplish
this difficult task, you will need to learn ways to "hear" and "see"
painful things about yourself. The worksheets at the end of this
chapter will guide you in this work. Your pride is bound to get in
the way, especially when you are the only partner doing this. One

man disclosed, "When I think that what she said may be true, it feels like I've been kicked in the stomach."

Note that if you have always denied all your partner's accusations, it will require much more effort to acknowledge where you have been at fault. As one woman said, "It's a matter of pride now. After so vigorously defending what I did, how can I now admit he was right after all?" If you have not defended yourself, it will be easier (although never easy) to acknowledge your own contribution to your problems. This is another important benefit of not responding reactively.

The techniques outlined in the worksheets at the end of this chapter will help you to evaluate yourself. Try to see beyond the viciousness of your partner's attack, and look at its actual content. Then confront yourself by asking awkward and uncomfortable questions. If you really are behaving the way your partner says, and if you keep behaving this way, the outcome will continue to be poor. Remember that it takes a strong person to admit to being wrong and then to do something about it. And even if you end this relationship, you may eventually enter into another one, and you will carry your problem behavior and its consequences with you. If you are unsure of the validity of what you have been accused of, you can look for some signs. For example, you can talk to friends or family members who will be honest with you rather than telling you only what you want to hear. Or you can closely observe yourself over time.

You will need to make a concerted effort to observe yourself honestly rather than automatically dismissing anything painful that was said to you. If you find it too difficult to admit to your partner that you are guilty of the problem behavior you were accused of, you can still try to change the behavior. One man described his efforts in this way: "My wife accused me of undermining her in public. I eventually got to the point where I didn't attack her when she brought it up. Then I began to wonder if it was true. After a while, I noticed how my 'humor' was, in reality, a subtle put-down."

This kind of self-honesty always has a powerfully positive effect on a relationship. Since only the same few problem patterns are repeated in a relationship, resolving any one will have a profound and cumulative impact. Don't treat this lightly; both your relationship and your own happiness will be deeply affected by whether or not you decide to follow through. Remember that while this approach will not force your partner to change instantly, it *can* open up communication to allow issues to be discussed without turmoil or hostility. Only after this point has been reached can your contentious issues be resolved. If, after working on the issue of blame, a problem still remains between you, the next chapters will help guide you to a resolution.

## FAULT AND BLAME WORKSHEETS

*You may wish to make several photocopies of the following pages while they are still blank, since you may be repeating these exercises several times.*

After reading about fault and blame, you will now have some idea of how these issues are creating a wedge between you and your partner. To resolve these issues, it will be helpful to have a goal. Describe below what you aim to change. (For example, "My goal is to eliminate the emotional upsets that result every time one of us comments to the other about something they did wrong.")

_____

_____

_____

## OBSERVING FAULT-FINDING AND BLAMING

Reread chapter 6 from the section Making Observations (page 117) on, to help guide your efforts here.

1. First, to help you identify fault-finding and blaming interactions, describe an occasion of fault-finding that you observed between two other people. (For example, "At work, my colleague raised the issue of an error someone made in an accusatory and insulting way. The offended person immediately got into an old brain reaction, didn't hear anything that was said, and a big argument ensued.")

_____

_____

_____

## OBSERVING YOUR PARTNER'S FAULT-FINDING

Blaming can be very obvious or very subtle. This next set of exercises is designed to help you identify your partner's blaming behavior as a step toward discovering how you find fault with your partner.

1. Does your partner blame you openly by saying something is your fault, or indirectly by implying it in the way certain words are spoken? Please check:

Openly  ☐                              Indirectly  ☐

2. Identify the issues this fault-finding deals with, for example, money, the condition of the house.

_____

_____

_____

3. Describe in detail how this occurs. (For example, "Whenever something goes wrong with our car, he never comes right out and says it's my fault. But he has oodles of reasons why it couldn't possibly be his fault, and his line of reasoning ends up pointing to me as the one to blame.")

_____

_____

_____

4. Sometimes a blaming attitude is revealed by specific words. Check off which of these words your partner uses in blaming you.
Tells me I am:

At *fault*                      ☐          To *blame*          ☐
Responsible for what
   *happened*          ☐

5. Describe how often your partner uses these words and about which issues. (For example, "Whenever our checking account doesn't balance, she says 'It's your fault,' even though we've agreed it's her responsibility to balance it.")

_____

_____

_____

6. The following exercises will help you see the provocative way your partner discusses contentious issues, finding fault and blaming you.

List the "you" statements your partner makes. (For example, "Whenever he gets upset he says, 'If you'd done what you were supposed to do, this wouldn't have happened.'")

_____

_____

_____

7. To see more clearly how often these "you" statements are made, record below the dates your partner made them.

_____

_____

_____

8. Check off the ways your partner's "you" statements provoked you.

The tone of voice                  ☐          The loudness of voice        ☐
The negative motives                           The provocative words
   imputed to me               ☐             used                                 ☐
The number of times my
   partner repeated
   statements                    ☐
Other(s)

_____

_____

_____

9. Check off how your partner tried to avoid being thought at fault.
My partner:

| | | | |
|---|---|---|---|
| Misinterpreted what I meant | ☐ | Ignored me | ☐ |
| Did not hear me | ☐ | Claimed to have misheard me | ☐ |
| Rationalized his actions | ☐ | Gave excuses | ☐ |
| Distorted what I said | ☐ | Evaded responsibility | ☐ |
| Lied about what occurred | ☐ | Changed the subject | ☐ |
| Justified his actions | ☐ | Denied responsibility | ☐ |
| | | Other(s) | |

_____

_____

_____

10. After avoiding responsibility, most likely your partner attacked you. Check off how the attack occurred.
My partner:

| | | | |
|---|---|---|---|
| Manipulated/pressured me | ☐ | Tried to confuse me | ☐ |
| Sulked/withdrew | ☐ | Directly attacked me | ☐ |
| Other(s) | | | |

_____

_____

_____

11. Describe in detail all the responses you checked. (For example, "My boyfriend tried to confuse me by bringing up something I did in the past that had nothing to do with what we were discussing.")

_____

_____

_____

12. Describe how you feel when your partner finds fault with you in this way. (For example, "When she implied I left the side of the crib down on

purpose, I felt so hurt, and I questioned how could she love me as she says she does.")

_____

_____

_____

13. If you defended yourself against your partner's attack, check off how you did so.

| | | | |
|---|---|---|---|
| Repeatedly explained my position | ☐ | Tried to reason with my partner | ☐ |
| Justified my position | ☐ | Answered the charges | ☐ |
| Sought approval for what I'd said | ☐ | Sought permission to present my position | ☐ |
| Attacked my partner's position | ☐ | Attacked my partner's personality | ☐ |

14. If you checked anything above, describe in detail how you defended yourself. (For example, "I reached a point where I answered all his ridiculing and false charges. Then I attacked him and his ridiculous views.")

_____

_____

_____

At the point described above, reactive infection occurred between you, and your own defensive response contributed to your partner's continuing attacks. Note that this is the point of greatest opportunity for putting an end to such attacks. By choosing not to defend your position, you will remove the fuel for further attack.

15. Describe the effect your partner's accusations are having on you and your relationship. (For example, "When she blames me about something where I know I'm not to blame, I hate myself for arguing back, and I hate her for blaming me to begin with.")

_____

_____

_____

16. Does your partner say she knows she's responsible for her own life, actions, and feelings, and yet, when she's upset, blames you for how she feels and behaves?
Yes ☐                                    No ☐

If you checked yes, focus on your partner's *behavior*, not words, as the indication of her true position. When you see an actual change in behavior, you will know that significant change has begun within.

You should now have a basic picture of how your partner avoids taking responsibility for her actions and tries to make you feel responsible for them. Keep adding to the above entries after examining further reactive occasions, to see this pattern more clearly.

## OBSERVING WHAT HAPPENS WITH YOUR OWN FAULT-FINDING

Now that you have some idea of your partner's blaming patterns, use the following exercises to understand your own.

1. Do you blame your partner directly, by saying he's at fault, or indirectly, perhaps insinuating it in your "reasoning?"
Directly ☐                        Indirectly ☐

2. Describe how you've done so. (For example, "The last time something went wrong, I didn't accuse him directly. Rather, I justified my behavior, implying I wasn't responsible and therefore he was.")

_____

_____

_____

3. Identify the topics or areas in which you find fault with your partner. (For example, "Around the children, money, problems with the car.")

_____

_____

_____

4. Check off the blaming words you used when speaking with your partner.
At *fault*   ☐      To *blame*   ☐      Responsible for what *happened*   ☐

The following exercises will help you see how using the word "you" causes problems for both your partner and your relationship.

5. Record any recent "you" statements made by you. (For example, "During our last disagreement, I made eight 'you' statements. I said, 'It was your fault this whole incident started. If you hadn't been so stupid, we wouldn't be in this predicament.'")

_____

_____

_____

6. Check off how your "you" statements were provocative. They were provocative because of:

The tone of voice I used   ☐          The loudness of my voice   ☐
The negative motives I                 The provocative words I
    ascribed to his actions   ☐            used                       ☐
The number of times I
    repeated statements   ☐            Other(s)

_____

_____

7. Record the dates you made such statements.

_____

_____

_____

8. Describe specifically how these "you" statements were made. (For example, "In the last three arguments, one time I was loud, another time biting, and another time I was loud, biting, and implied he didn't pay a bill because he was shiftless, rather than just forgetful.")

_____

_____

_____

9. As best you can, describe how you think your partner felt when you made fault-finding remarks. (For example, "I remember how it hurt me when she implied my mistakes were on purpose, rather than due to simple forgetfulness. It must hurt her just as much.")

_____

_____

_____

10. Do you believe you are responsible for what you feel and how you behave, yet when something went wrong you blamed your partner for what you were feeling and how you were behaving?

Yes ☐                    No ☐

If you answered yes, welcome to the human race! In my experience very few people's actions are entirely consistent with their words. So if you, too, are guilty of this inconsistency, don't become disheartened. Instead, strive to rectify it by taking responsibility for what you are now feeling and how you are behaving during stressful times.

11. Check off the things you did to avoid accepting responsibility.

| | | | |
|---|---|---|---|
| I misinterpreted what my partner said | ☐ | I misheard what my partner said | ☐ |
| I rationalized what I had done | ☐ | I distorted what my partner said | ☐ |
| I lied about what occurred | ☐ | I justified my actions | ☐ |
| I ignored what my partner said | ☐ | I didn't hear what my partner said | ☐ |
| I changed the subject | ☐ | I denied responsibility | ☐ |
| I denied having said or done what I really did say or do | ☐ | | |

12. After you had defended yourself, if you then attacked your partner in some way, check off how you did so.

| | | | |
|---|---|---|---|
| I sulked/withdrew | ☐ | I retaliated | ☐ |
| I tried to confuse my partner | ☐ | I tried to confuse the issue | ☐ |
| | | I manipulated/pressured my partner | ☐ |

13. Now describe in further detail the items you have checked. (For example, "After denying all he said to me, I tried to confuse the issue by twisting around what he said, to make him look at fault for our financial situation.")

_____

_____

_____

14. If you attacked your partner, check off how your partner reacted.

| | | |
|---|---|---|
| Repeatedly explained himself ☐ | Tried to reason with me ☐ | |
| | Justified what she said ☐ | |
| Answered my charges ☐ | Sought my approval for | |
| Sought my permission to | his viewpoints ☐ | |
| say it ☐ | Attacked my viewpoints ☐ | |
| Verbally attacked me ☐ | | |

At the point described above there was reactive infection, and you initiated the argument and division that followed. Blaming is a normal human reaction, so don't lose heart if you have seen yourself doing any of the above. Simply keep working on moving beyond blaming in the future.

15. Now describe the effect your attack had on you, your partner, and the relationship. (For example, "I felt horrible afterward, he was fearful of approaching me, and, as a couple, we became very distant for a considerable time.")

_____

_____

_____

16. How long did these effects last?
Minutes ☐     Hours ☐     Days ☐     Weeks ☐
Months ☐

Note: These exercises can rarely be filled out completely at one sitting, but will require repeated efforts. When you have done them, you will have begun to see how your own blaming behavior causes problems in your relationship and life, too. Please keep at it, because the more clearly this blaming pattern is seen, the easier it will be to change it.

## TALKING TO YOUR PARTNER WITHOUT BLAMING

1. Pick one of the topics or issues you identified above, in which you blamed your partner. Record it here. (For example, "I blamed my partner when I brought up the subject of how sloppy he is.")

_____

_____

_____

2. Describe how you blamed your partner. (For example, "I said to him, 'As sloppy as you are, you must think I'm your slave rather than your wife.' ")

_____

_____

_____

3. In contrast to the above, it is important that you learn to say what you think in an unprovocative, nonaccusatory way. The following exercise will help you accomplish this. Write your true "I" position on this subject. (For example, "I'm too tired to clean up after him. He should clean up after himself.")

_____

_____

_____

Now that you are clear about what you want to say, your next step is to plan for and work at saying it nonreactively. Though this was discussed earlier, it is worth repeating here: Do not make "you" statements.

Remember to mentally rehearse what you want to say and how to say it, until you can do it in exactly the way you want. Then write it down here. (For example, "The next time this issue comes up, I will say, 'I'm very tired/overworked, and will only be cleaning my own clothes from now on.'")

_____

_____

_____

## COPING WITH YOUR INNER RESISTANCE AND FAILURES

The anti-change forces within you will have compelled you to act on your "right" to vent your feelings and to blame your partner as you have always done, regardless of the negative outcome. But your pro-change forces will have encouraged you to use restraint and to follow through on your intended change.

1. Describe that inner struggle between whether or not to blame your partner. (For example, "One part of me says to cut her down, she deserves it! Another part reminds me of how that will only make the situation worse, and how I need to say what I planned.")

_____

_____

_____

2. Write here the pain you feel at not being able to express your feelings spontaneously. (For example, "It hurts to think that she is taking advantage of my good nature, and that I'm not telling her what I think of that and her.")

_____

_____

_____

It is very likely that initially your inner anti-change forces will win. As this is to be expected, don't lose hope when it happens. Rethink your plan and try again until eventually you are successful. Changing ingrained habits always takes time, but in the end you will succeed.

Though you now have planned the change in how you will speak to your partner, it is very likely that you will only remember your planned response *after* you become caught up in a reactive interaction. The following exercises are designed to help you in your attempts.

3. Check off each time you missed an opportunity to use your new way of speaking.

| | | |
|---|---|---|
| 1st missed opportunity | ☐ | 6th missed opportunity ☐ |
| 2nd missed opportunity | ☐ | 7th missed opportunity ☐ |

| | | | |
|---|---|---|---|
| 3rd missed opportunity | ☐ | 8th missed opportunity | ☐ |
| 4th missed opportunity | ☐ | 9th missed opportunity | ☐ |
| 5th missed opportunity | ☐ | 10th missed opportunity | ☐ |

Note: Don't look at these tries as failures, but as one step closer to success.

4. After these misses, you are likely to become aware of your reaction during the reactive encounter, while still being unable to change. Check off each time your efforts were still unsuccessful. Though not yet successful, you are close to it, so don't give up now! A little more effort and this problem will be resolved.

| | | | |
|---|---|---|---|
| 1st missed opportunity | ☐ | 6th missed opportunity | ☐ |
| 2nd missed opportunity | ☐ | 7th missed opportunity | ☐ |
| 3rd missed opportunity | ☐ | 8th missed opportunity | ☐ |
| 4th missed opportunity | ☐ | 9th missed opportunity | ☐ |
| 5th missed opportunity | ☐ | 10th missed opportunity | ☐ |

The last step was accomplished when your attempt to change became successful. When this happened, you eliminated a recurring problem in your relationship and your life. Congratulations!

After enjoying this victory, you can go back to resolve another problem area where you have been blaming your partner. Remember that the first attempt is always the most difficult, and succeeding efforts will become increasingly easier.

## ANTICIPATING YOUR PARTNER'S BLAMING RESPONSES

Now you will learn how to stop your partner from blaming you. This will involve dealing with your partner's efforts to blame you further when you refuse to accept unjust blame. The exercises in this section are designed to anticipate and address this response. Please try to keep in mind that your partner's behavior is a normal reactive response to change, not something done maliciously by a bad or evil person.

1. Describe one situation in which your partner blames you. It is important to be very specific about what your partner says. (For example, "Whenever we get on the subject of how I don't want him to lie to me

any longer, he says, 'I do it for your own good. It's best you don't know about certain things, because you couldn't handle it.' ")

———————————————————————————

———————————————————————————

———————————————————————————

You now have a clearer picture of how he blames you in this particular situation.

2. Describe how you typically react to this kind of attack. (For example, "I try to reason and remind him about all the times he's lied to me.")

———————————————————————————

———————————————————————————

———————————————————————————

3. To keep yourself from becoming reactive to being blamed, you must steer through your partner's blame, evasions, denials, and attacks without allowing yourself to become engaged (much like a boxer bobs and weaves to keep his opponent from landing any punches).

Do not try to reason, justify, placate, attack, convince, or punish your partner. Simply express your "I" position—nothing more.

Once you have clarified your position to yourself, you must express it in the form of an intention or choice. Write down exactly what you will say. (For example, "I do not want to be lied to any more.")

When this subject comes up again I will say

———————————————————————————

———————————————————————————

———————————————————————————

4. Once you have stated your position on the issue, your partner will nonetheless attempt to blame you. Anticipating such reactions will be very helpful to you. Try writing them down first in pencil; then you can change them if they turn out to be different. Here is a partial list.
My partner will:

| Accuse/attack me | ☐ | Ignore me/ignore my view | ☐ |
| Attack what I said | ☐ | Retaliate | ☐ |

| | | |
|---|---|---|
| Attempt to make me | Be critical of me | ☐ |
| feel guilty or wrong ☐ | Pressure/manipulate me to | |
| | change | ☐ |

5. Your partner will first try to draw you into defending yourself, and most likely you will eventually do so through sheer exhaustion. Don't worry; it is rare that this does not happen at the beginning.

Here is a list of the ways most of us defend ourselves. In pencil, check off which things you believe you will do. Afterward, in ink, check off how you actually defended yourself.

| | | | |
|---|---|---|---|
| I repeatedly explained | | I justified my position | ☐ |
| my position | ☐ | I answered the charges | ☐ |
| I sought approval for | | I attacked my partner's | |
| what I'd said | ☐ | viewpoints | ☐ |
| I attacked my partner's | | I sought permission to | |
| personality | ☐ | present my viewpoint | ☐ |
| I tried to reason with my | | | |
| partner | ☐ | | |

6. Describe how you will refrain from defending yourself in the future. (For example, "When my partner attacks what I say, instead of attacking him back, I will tell him I have nothing further to say about it.")

_____

_____

_____

7. If your partner continues attacking (which is highly likely), you will need to disengage yourself to keep from reacting, as discussed in chapter 3. Describe how you will break off contact. (For example, "I will go into the next room.")

_____

_____

_____

8. Describe how you think your partner will try to prevent you from breaking off contact. (For example, "She will follow me into the next room, pound on the wall, hide my car keys.")

_____

_____

_____

9. As well as reacting with immediate provocation, there is a strong possibility that your partner will retaliate over the long term. It will help to anticipate this as best you can. Describe how you think this could occur. (For example, "She will spend too much money. Sleep in the spare bedroom. Refuse to visit my family next Christmas.")

_____

_____

_____

10. How long do you think this retaliation will last?
Hours ☐      Days ☐      Weeks ☐

Following is a list of Do's and Don'ts that you may want to refer to occasionally.

| Do | Don't |
|---|---|
| State your own view. | Try to "sell" your view or justify it. |
| Keep your own perspective. | Lose hope. (Failures are to be expected.) |
| Vent your feelings to a trusted friend. | Vent your feelings to your partner. |
| Disengage as soon as you become reactive. | Regard your partner's behavior as unique. |
| Try to learn from your failed efforts. | Give up. |
| Stick to your plan. | Bring up the past. |
| Try to anticipate your partner's reactions. | Point to or be led down the road of who "started" it or who's to blame. |
| Rehearse your planned changes. | |
| Stay focused on the present. | |

It's rare to be successful immediately in this challenging endeavor. But I have found that most people do succeed after repeated attempts and after they have learned from their previous efforts.

As discussed before, you will go through various stages as you implement your plan. But if you persevere, working your way through each stage, you will in the end be successful in your efforts. Then, after taking a much deserved break, you can go back and do the same thing in another problem area.

# CHAPTER 7

# Using Your Anger
# Constructively

If you have expressed your anger to your partner, and his or her behavior has not changed, you will probably still be angry. This chapter explores what to do with your anger while its source remains. Although it is valuable to openly express your anger in some situations, in many others it is not. Certainly, during a reactive exchange is not a good time if you want your situation to improve. Expressing it in a controlled way after both partners have calmed down is better, but many times this will not be productive either. Often, the problem remains, and continuing to make your anger known will not end it or the emotional drain it causes to everyone involved. The following situations are typical examples of what can happen.

A woman was constantly angry at her husband because he would not set limits with his ex-wife. He immediately acceded to all of his ex-wife's wishes, as when she suddenly asked him to take the children for the weekend; his partner then felt slighted because her own plans had to be changed. Though she discussed this with him and vented her considerable anger about the situation, he told her he could not do anything else. The situation continued, along with her growing resentment.

A man who had been in therapy for five years had become aware of the anger he felt toward those around him. But once in touch with the anger, he began to vent it on his wife, his grown children, and the rest of his family. This made him feel better, but he also found that everyone was retreating from him, fearful that they might set him off again. Thus, the relief he felt from releasing his anger was more than offset by the loneliness he felt when everyone avoided him.

Another woman spent many years trying to get her husband more involved with the children and herself, but he defeated her at every turn. She was angry at him all the time, and let him know it. However, as well as making their life together even more exhausting, her anger was eating her up. She still loved him and did not want to divorce him. "What do I do about my anger?" was the question she posed.

All of these people share the common dilemma of what to do with their anger. When they do not vent it, it drains them emotionally and physically. When they do release it, the result is either reactive confrontations, which are even more exhausting, or alienation from their partners. Getting in touch with and expressing their anger does not improve their lives or their relationships. Instead it both reinforces their anger and worsens their situations. Clearly, an alternative is needed.

## The Ways Anger is Expressed

To understand the variety of ways anger is expressed, besides shouting or screaming, we need to become aware of its other forms. It can, for example, be conveyed simply by tone of voice. (As one man said, "When she's angry, she never raises her voice. Instead, her tone is very biting.") Or by not saying anything. (As another man said, "She ignores me until she's over whatever it is that she's mad about.") Or by bodily reactions. (As, for example, people whose ulcers "act up" when they get angry, or who have headaches, or who start shaking when they become angry.) Others may only show their anger with some sort of delayed behavior. (As one woman said, "I can tell when he's mad at me. He stays out later with his friends or at work." Or as one husband said of his wife, "She goes out and spends money we don't have. That's a sure-fire clue she's mad at me over something.")

There are also different degrees of anger, such as unresolved anger that turns into resentment, and when this is not resolved, becomes bitterness. Anger, of course, is an old brain reaction and provides much of the fuel for reactivity. Like all reactive behavior, unless it is dealt with directly, it grows. It is set off by an emotional trigger of some kind leading to such physiological changes as the heart speeding up, adrenaline being released into the system, and blood vessels constricting as the body goes into its fight-or-flight mode. At the same time, rational thought is overtaken by an overwhelming urge for the satisfaction of a reactive encounter—a disagreement or fight—regardless of future consequences and costs. This is followed by the reactive infection stage, where one partner tries to provoke the other, which in turn is followed by escalation. It can also become progressive, as for the woman who said, "I'm at the point where I'm constantly angry at him over nothing."

Whether it is suppressed or expressed, we pay a heavy price for our unresolved anger. It blocks effective communication with our partners, prevents problem-solving, and erodes the caring. It also tends to take over our lives in general, and may lead to the further pain of remorse. Sometimes it can even lead to violence, as for the man who hits his wife or the woman who throws things at her husband.

Anger can also lead to physical effects, such as sleeplessness or a loss of appetite. It often leads to the pursuit of destructive distractions, such as drinking or overspending. Anger also raises one's level of stress and unhappiness. Contrary to popular belief, time does not always dissipate anger, and one may still be angry about things that were said or done twenty-five years ago. That is why venting anger—even at the appropriate person—is not always the best option.

## A Common Source of Anger

If we look closely at where anger originates, we see that its source often lies in our expectations. When we expect or anticipate something and it does not materialize, disappointment follows and our hurt is transformed into anger which, if not resolved, usually turns into resentment, and can over time, develop into bitterness. Anger is such a powerful old brain reaction that when we experience it, we forget that its origin was in our unmet expectations, disappointments, and hurt feelings.

From the day we are born, we absorb expectations of what should be and could be from many different sources. Some come from the larger society (men should be tough, women should be soft); some from our cultural group (in Irish families, you are expected to be stoical; in Italian ones, expressive); some come from our families (the eldest child should excel). Sometimes these have been transmitted verbally, as when a child is told to do her best in school, but more often they are conveyed nonverbally so that we remain unaware of them. The only evidence that we have these expectations comes from the anger we feel when they are not met. All relationships, particularly those with problems, are accompanied by unspoken lists of what "should be," ranging from who is expected to take out the garbage, to more significant expectations about honesty and fidelity. Many people have so many expectations of their partners that they live their lives in a dream of what they feel should be, rather than in the reality of what is. As long as their expectations remain unfulfilled, they feel disappointed, hurt, and angry, all the while waiting for their dream to materialize. This common experience was well described by one woman when she said,

> The past eight years I've expected my husband to be more talkative and involved. He wasn't that way when I dated him, but I lived with the hope that some day he would be. When it finally hit me that he never was and never would be more involved, I realized I loved a man who only existed in my dreams and hopes, rather than in reality.

## Thinking Our Expectations Are Entitlements
Few other rights are seen to be as indisputable as the right to expect certain things of our partner and to get angry when they are not forthcoming. Yet, while most of us feel entitled to expect things

from our partners, we resent it when our partners make their own demands. Expectations are not bad in themselves. To the contrary, it is normal and healthy to have expectations of others and of life. Many of these are inalienable rights, such as the right to be treated decently, to be spoken to with civility, not to be cheated or lied to, to name a few. However, they may become a problem when we adhere so unbendingly to them that we fail to look beyond to how they may be causing complications in our lives. A common response to this is to say, "But my expectations are reasonable. I don't think it's asking too much to expect certain things of my partner, such as being honest with me. It's only fair." And, certainly, it is not asking too much. But whether or not our expectations are reasonable and fair is not the issue here. The primary issue is how these expectations impact our lives. Are they helpful to our life and relationship or are they destructive? Do they ultimately contribute to our happiness and to getting along better with our partner or to the opposite?

A man had been married for thirty-six years to a very distant, domineering, and cruelly sarcastic wife. Throughout the years he always expected to be treated better. "It's not expecting too much, is it?" he would ask me, and I would reply, "It certainly isn't." However, because that expectation was neither met nor abandoned, the anger it produced turned first into resentment and then into bitterness. Eventually, he turned to tranquilizers. He was certainly absolutely justified in expecting decent treatment from his partner. But had he accepted that his wife would never treat him any better, it would have freed him from his paralysis and inaction. Though it was quite reasonable, the cost of expecting better treatment hardly proved to have been worthwhile.

Since anger is an old brain reaction, regardless of whether or not it is about a fair expectation, its impact is progressive and must be dealt with before you feel like the man who said, "Nothing is left in me or our relationship except my resentments toward her." As long as our expectations remain unmet, they continue to fuel our anger. Time does not take care of this, nor will releasing the anger do anything more than provide temporary relief. Lowering our expectations is the only thing that will actually eliminate that anger.

## *Evaluating Your Expectations*

If you are at a point in your life and relationship where you have tried expressing your anger and have not found it helpful to your situation, then you have only three viable options. You can continue to smolder in your anger, you can lower your unmet expectations, or you can leave the relationship. If you don't want to leave your partner, that means you must choose one of the other two. And both of these are painful.

The course most frequently followed is to wait for the anger to go away by itself or for the partner to finally change in response to this anger. While this seems to require less effort, it is also based on an illusion—a false hope, which will only produce further disappointment, hurt, and anger. But if you have decided to rid yourself of unresolved anger with its negative effects, and to work to transform your relationship, the rest of this chapter and the worksheets that follow will help you do this.

Lowering your expectations will not immediately change your partner. Instead, it will produce a profound letdown, which is both painful and humbling. When you are humbled in this way you can no longer deceive yourself, and you are able to accomplish something very significant that you were unable to do before. You can honestly reevaluate both your relationship and yourself. An example of this was a woman of forty-five, married to a domineering, verbally abusive, and self-centered husband. She had lived for the past eighteen years of her marriage without doing anything about it. Her expectation that some day he would stop his domineering behavior allowed her to endure it year after year. But when she lowered her expectation, realizing that he would always be like this, she started seeing her situation more realistically. In her own words:

> Soon after I got married, I saw he wasn't the person I expected. I never dealt with that because I kept expecting and hoping this would be the week, month, year he would come around. As a result, I kept excusing, overlooking, rationalizing, and therefore putting up with his poor treatment.

Lowering our expectations forces us to deal with the reality of a relationship by puncturing fantasies and slowly, painfully bringing us back to reality. Another example of this was the man whose girlfriend of four years was spiteful, manipulative, and deceitful. He reported,

> I learned how to talk to her about it without attacking her, but she didn't change. I got angry about it, but that only made her more spiteful and deceptive. When I changed my expectations and began to expect her to remain this way, I finally saw the relationship as it truly was. I didn't have the close relationship I thought I had. In fact, it was horrendous. At that point, I realized I needed to make some long overdue changes, like stop excusing her behavior in the hope it would disappear by itself.

Because we tend to be aware only of our partner's faults, while remaining unaware of our own, we become convinced that we contribute little or nothing to our relationship's problems but are innocent victims of our partner's behavior. Lowering our expectations forces us to see our own faults as well and allows us to move toward a solution. The following couple's relationship is an example of this process.

For many years, the wife and husband stayed angry at one another about the same issues. She complained about his "cheapness," his criticisms of the children, and his refusal to stand up to his family's attacks on her. He complained about her "meddlesome" family, her lack of involvement with him, and her "spoiling" the children. To no avail, each repeatedly vented their anger at the other's behavior. When they finally lowered their expectations of each other, they began to focus intensely on themselves for the first time in many years. She had come to the realization that he, an accountant, was never going to earn the money required to support the lifestyle she had expected. She also had come to accept that his way of disciplining their children was always going to be harsher and more demanding than her own. And last, and by far the hardest, she had come to terms with the fact that, for whatever reason, he was never going to stand up to his family on her behalf.

He, on the other hand, had to lower his expectations for her independence from her family and had to accept that he came second to them in her life. In the same way that she had had to do, he had to accept that her child-rearing methods would never change. Then, as both were able to lower their expectations, each became increasingly aware of their own irresponsibilities and inconsistencies. She realized she was, in fact, spoiling the children, ignoring her husband, and putting her own family before him, as he had been telling her all this time. She also realized that he had been justified in his criticism of her for being a nag about money. He discovered he was, indeed, stingy with his wife, overly critical of the children, and did let his parents attack his wife needlessly. He came to realize that he was not providing the attention and support that she needed, so she was turning to her family for it. Along with this came her understanding that as long as she needed her family in this way, he would always play a less important role in her life than she wanted. By focusing on their own shortcomings, each learned that the other had had a great deal of justification for their complaints. Fortunately for this couple, lowering their expectations eliminated their anger and problems entirely.

For others who are aware of their shortcomings but lack the motivation to correct them, lowering their expectations of their partners provides an impetus for change. One man put it like this:

> My heart was never in my efforts to change, because some part of me always clung to the hope that my wife would change and that my marriage and life would improve without my having to work to make it better. When I finally gave up that hope, I realized my situation wouldn't improve until I did something to improve it. At that point, I was able to follow through on changing.

And for those who have put up an emotional wall to prevent themselves feeling any further hurt and anger, lowering their expectations also lowers this wall. They are forced to deal with their hurts, disappointments, and resentments, which, once faced, allow healing to begin and closeness to develop.

## What Our Expectations Accomplish

Many people believe that if we do not have high expectations of others, they will offer very little in return. While this may be true in some social settings, in a close relationship the opposite occurs. The

less we expect of our partners (and the more we expect of ourselves), the more we receive, although this may not be what we had
originally wanted. For example, a man who for many years had expected his wife to be more involved with him was angered by her
aloofness. But when he resolved to accept that she was always going
to be uninvolved, he began to see himself more clearly; he saw the
reason for her uninvolvement was that he was too "clingy." At that
point, he was able to work on becoming less smothering with her,
and she responded by being less aloof. In contrast, another man saw
his partner's refusal to be involved with him as only the tip of the
iceberg. His relationship was in much poorer shape than he had
been willing to admit, and he now saw that she took advantage of
his easygoing nature. His solution to the problem was to be less tol-
erant of many of her actions.

When an attitude of "expect nothing, get nothing" dominates a
relationship, it indicates that there are a significant number of problems. In such situations, either the tasks at hand do not get done, or
if they do, the resulting emotional climate makes the cost prohibi-
tive. When people genuinely care for each other, they do not do
something because it is expected or demanded of them, but because
the emotion they feel makes them glad to do it. Only after the love
begins to fade (through reactivity, blaming, and so on) do people
stop doing something for their partner unless it is angrily demanded. In this scenario, the job may get done but it also makes
closeness between a couple impossible. What is needed to improve
these situations is a significant change in the basis on which the relationship is built, which always involves changing expectations.
Thus, by not expressing anger (though not suppressing it or stew-
ing in it, either), it becomes possible to ultimately improve the relationship significantly.

Often it is the more submissive people-pleasers who read this
type of book. And these people also often have difficulty following
through on change. When upset, they tend to vent their anger,
which may help them feel better in the short run, but saps their motivation to make changes that would benefit them in the long run. In
this case, anger turned inward can motivate someone to follow
through on changing. Contrary to common belief, this anger need

not cause depression. Only unresolved inward anger will cause depression. When used to mobilize change in behavior, it will bring relief, as well as improve self-esteem, both of which will prevent depression. One man described this process in this way: "For years I was a dormouse with my wife. I said nothing, but seethed over what was bothering me. Finally, I got angry enough at myself for taking it, and now I'm speaking up for myself. I feel better about myself than I have in twenty years." Similarly, a woman whose husband remained evasive over whether or not his affair was over finally became angry at herself rather than at him. This gave her the strength to not accept his evasions any longer. As she put it: "That's when I got strong enough not to let him treat me that way any longer."

When unresolved anger about your expectations is a large part of your life and relationship, rather than seeking new ways to get your partner to meet those expectations or new ways to vent that anger, the most constructive thing to do is to use your unresolved anger to challenge your expectations of your partner.

## Becoming Aware of Your Anger and Expectations

The first step toward improvement is to increase your awareness of the unfulfilled expectations that dominate your life and relationship. Because so many expectations are assimilated unknowingly, they may play a bigger part in your life than you realize. It may be easier to observe this at first in someone else, so in the worksheets you will start by identifying signs of your partner's anger and then observing your own reaction to it. Perhaps you become defiant, or you ignore it, or you get angry and snap back. Perhaps you try to appease your partner. Later, you will observe the toll these reactions take on you and your relationship. In spite of what is professed about "openness" to anger, if the anger is repetitive, it leads to a negative response, and eventually tends to break the emotional bonds that bind two people to each other.

After you have sensitized yourself to the effect your unresolved anger is having on your relationship, you will shift your focus to your unfulfilled expectations. Then, the harder you push yourself to see and deal with these, the greater the improvements will be. This is especially true of unconscious expectations, and you will become aware of them by using the observation process described in the worksheets. Instead of venting your anger, you will mobilize it to identify your unspoken and implied expectations. You will trace the anger you feel back through the hurt and disappointment to its origin. The following examples of typical relationship expectations may help you identify your own.

A woman was continually angry about her husband's lack of dependability and failure to ask or show concern about how she was doing. She traced her increasing rage to her expectation that he would be considerate and caring. Another woman was filled with resentment that her partner let her drive their car when he knew it was in poor mechanical shape. She felt hurt that he was not more concerned about her physical safety and thought it represented his lack of caring. One man was angry for many years because his wife had not been the kind of mother he had expected. He thought she was critical and overprotective of their children. He had ranted and raved at her about it for many years, but continued to expect her to change. Another woman resented her husband's lack of responsibility around their house. For example, she expected him to fix the leaking roof. When, as usual, he did not fix it, her expectations were disappointed and she felt angry again. Another man continued to feel resentful toward his stepchildren because his wife did not want to have children with him. His unfulfilled expectations for children of his own were the source of his anger at his stepchildren. One woman resented her boyfriend, but was unclear why. Eventually, she traced her anger to her boyfriend's refusal to get a better job. If he got a better job, she would not have to work and could devote all her efforts to raising their children as she had always wanted and expected to do.

## Resolving Your Anger

What is described here and in the worksheets will apply only to areas where your anger is causing an ongoing problem. Since anger is a form of old brain reactive behavior, your first step will be to learn to manage your out-of-control anger. This is because nothing constructive can be accomplished in this state. Once you have identified the expectations that are giving rise to your repeated anger, you will begin to address the expectations themselves. Perhaps you are angry at your partner for being inconsiderate, unappreciative, moody, disrespectful, selfish, verbally abusive. Perhaps you are angry about your partner's affairs, financial irresponsibility, relationship with the children, alcohol, gambling. You may be angry because your partner is cold, distant, and unloving. Instead of expecting this behavior to change, you must start thinking along the lines that your partner may not change. (It is safe to assume that if the disturbing behavior has been going on for some time, it is unlikely to change by itself.)

Thus, instead of expecting your partner to appreciate you more, consider that you will never be appreciated again. Instead of expecting that soon your partner will stop drinking, having affairs, being moody, blaming you for everything, or siding with the children against you, start to think that the behavior will never stop. If the problem is lack of respect, expect disrespect always. If you are unsure that your partner loves you, consider that he or she may not love you and never will again. Whether or not you expect your partner to change is not what will bring about a change. Here, the issue is for you to reclaim the control over your own life that you have lost because of your unfulfilled expectations and the resultant emotions.

## *Inner Repercussions of Letting Go of Expectations*
The longer an expectation is unfulfilled, the more it becomes an unattainable dream based on self-deception. When we lower our expectations, we grieve for the loss of that dream and tend to feel cheated out of something highly valued and desired. Sometimes our initial reaction to this letdown is hostility. Usually this anger is short-lived and is followed by grieving, confusion, despair, and hopelessness. We do not immediately feel better when we first lower our expectations but actually feel worse. Remember, it is only in this acutely painful, confused, and despairing state that personal reevaluation and change, followed by improvement, can take place. We will go through a substantial period of uncertainty and indeci-

sion before any improvement occurs. Below are some descriptions
of the painful emotions experienced during this period.

> CONFUSION: "I'm not sure what I believe in any more. I have a
> difficult time making decisions in my life where I didn't before."
> LONELINESS: "I feel all alone, even in the presence of others. I'm
> afraid I will always feel this lonely."
> EMPTINESS: "I feel so empty inside. It feels like I have a big hole in-
> side of me. I feel like a nothing; so meaningless."
> HOPELESSNESS, HELPLESSNESS: "What I hoped for will never be.
> What is the sense of trying any more? Maybe I should just give up.
> Will I survive this?"
> FAILURE: "All the things I had hoped for were just a pipe dream. I
> feel so stupid."
> EMOTIONALLY DRAINED: "I feel no enthusiasm. I feel lifeless,
> tired, and drained. I feel like I've died inside."
> UNCARED FOR: "I feel unloved and unlovable. I wish someone
> cared about me, just me, the way I am. But nobody cares about me
> or appreciates me."

The confusion, anger, and despair felt during this time are a sure
sign that change is taking place. They are not a punishment, nor are
they signs that something is wrong with, or unique to, you. Rather,
they are a necessary stage in going from what is not working in your
life to what will work in your future. And, in that regard, they represent a step forward. It is here, when you are hurting acutely, that
your focus shifts from your partner to yourself. At this point of realization you can begin to find the solution to your problems.

### The Point of Realization
When we reevaluate our lives from a position of confusion, emptiness, and loneliness, the door is also opened to a profound reevaluation of ourselves and our relationships. Only in this state can our
self-deception be stripped away and a clearer perception become
possible. For example, a woman had been choked with resentment
over her husband's never sharing his thoughts. After realizing that

he might never share them, she hit bottom. But in that abyss she said, "I never realized how difficult I make it for my husband to say anything that disagrees with me, how attacking I am." And a man who had been overly dependent on his wife could finally see his own clinging dependency, and found a new strength to do something about it. He described it thus: "I couldn't take another minute of my agony, so I finally started to become more independent. I had been saying I needed to do that for a long time, but I couldn't do it before. " Because they had believed they were right, their minds had become fixed, and they had been blinded to their own behavior.

Because of our rigidity, the prelude to change is always profound confusion and inner turmoil, which shake up our established perceptions and open us to new perceptions and viewpoints. Our fantasy hope fuels self-deception and, conversely, the hopelessness we feel when we recognize and moderate our unfulfilled expectations becomes the fuel for reevaluation and significant change. Thus, a woman whose partner was having affairs let go of her expectations and was then able to see that she had been critical, possessive, and cold. And that had likely contributed to her partner seeking female companionship elsewhere.

## Coping with the Pains of Change

Since the initial letdown can be very painful and the empty feelings lengthy and draining, it is important to keep some perspective about what you must go through during this time. Your pain is due to the death of your self-deception, which will allow a new and better life to emerge. However, make no mistake about it, this process is frightening, for it will confront you with your own shortcomings and failures. You may ask, "What should I do about the emptiness and loneliness I feel?" The answer is: Do nothing! Do not run from it or try to fill it. Instead, experience it by letting it sweep over you. It is similar to dealing with the death of someone close by crying over it, talking about it, sweating and stumbling through it as best we can. Other than that, we do nothing there, too. You are dealing with grief over the loss of your dream. While in other problem areas it is important to act, here you must not. Just sit with it as best you can. Work at getting behind the anger to the hurt, disappointment, and finally the loss you feel. When you accept this loss, you will also eliminate your anger. Until that point, your anger will continue.

Approach these feelings very, very slowly, taking increasing doses over time. When you feel overwhelmed, back off for the time being by getting your mind onto something else. Go slowly or stop when you feel too indecisive, confused, or despairing. Let yourself slowly adjust, just as your body does to allergy shots. Early on, self-pity and depression will be your almost constant companions, so it is critical to stay in touch with people during this time. Visit your friends and family to talk to them or just to be with them. You have gone too far into your feelings if you have withdrawn, spent excessive time in bed, have had suicidal thoughts, or are emotionally paralyzed. Most people need a long time to grieve for something deeply cherished—in this case, the loss of a long-held and deeply valued fantasy. As a general rule, the bigger the fantasy and the longer it was held, the more time it is likely to take to give it up. It would be nice if self-deception could be quickly replaced with reality, but according to my experience that does not happen. There is, however, a bright side to this: the emptiness will ultimately provide room for new perceptions, which will lead to realistic hope and tremendous improvement.

You will find that fantasy does not give up easily, but fights for its continued existence. You will experience many ups and downs in the days and weeks as fantasy and reality struggle for dominance. As one woman reported, "One day I feel fine, the next I can't get out of bed." You will also find your expectations rising again, together with the reemergence of your anger. One man expressed this very well: "It is really difficult to give up on what might have been. Especially when I don't have anything to replace it with. I get so angry when I think of it!" The woman who had expected her husband to fix things in their house came to the conclusion she would have to make the repairs herself or hire someone. But when she did them herself, after twenty years of waiting and fuming, she then became angry because her husband did not offer to help. When this happens to you, you can use this anger to track down the expectation that is giving rise to it and work to let go of the expectation.

### Changing Your Own Behavior

As you lower your expectations of your partner, you must raise your expectations of yourself. Having accepted that the problem is not going away, you must ask yourself what *you* are going to do about it and whether you are willing to settle for this situation. One man described his thoughts at this point: "I accepted that my wife wasn't going to stop sleeping around. But I wasn't going to let it control my life and make me sick any longer. I decided to get on with my life." Such changes of our habitual behavior take intense effort, but anger can supply that energy. Use the anger you still feel as fuel for the strength to change. Stop wasting this valuable energy by simply venting it when experience shows you that this will not resolve the problem. One man, whose wife continued in her lying, explained, "When I finally got mad enough at myself for putting up with it so long, I got on with my life."

Lowering our expectations is so frightening because it forces us to look at and deal with our own failures. In the short run, it seems a lot easier to avoid this and to continue to blame and vent our anger at our partner. In choosing to do so, however, we must be aware that this will cause our anger to become progressively worse. Though we naturally will think, "Why go through all of this? Why not just avoid it?", the fact is we have no choice in the matter, because we are dealing with reality. We may try to avoid dealing with it, but reality nonetheless will deal with us. Your only options are to put the pain you feel to constructive use, thus removing it, or to stretch it out over the rest of your life. Lowering your expectations of your partner will help you leave the pain behind. The rewards will be great, though your efforts to achieve them will undoubtedly be painful and take considerable time.

### Being on the Receiving End of Anger

Appeasement is our most common reaction to someone else's anger. The dictionary defines it as "giving in to the demands of . . ."

Clearly, appeasing anger does not work. Appeasement is an old brain reaction to anger and tends to fuel it rather than decrease it, while nonengagement will defeat it. About this issue people say such things as: "The more I give in, the more I have to give in," and "I'm afraid to bring things up because of her temper."

People who have difficulty with controlling their anger rarely initiate counseling. When they finally do seek help because of the upheavals it is causing in their relationship, their progress is slow. On the other hand, those who are on the receiving end of anger tend to progress much more quickly because their motivation is higher. As with all reactive behavior, our power lies not in changing our partner's anger, but in gradually learning how to stop appeasing.

A word about violence. Violence is an out-of-control, old brain behavior that is beyond the scope of this book. It is a volatile expression of anger and, like all reactive behavior, it is progressive. The more it happens, the more it will recur. And over time it will occur more intensely. With this extreme, out-of-control reactive kind of behavior, reasoning, appeasing, pleading, or attacking is futile. Hoping it will go away on its own only makes it worse. Instead, a more powerful force needs to be invoked—the law. Find out what you have to do where you live to get a temporary restraining order. Then get one, and *do not* drop it no matter how many assurances, promises, and apologies you get. Often the violent partner will "reform" temporarily in response to the immediate consequences imposed by the court but will revert to the old behavior as soon as those consequences are removed. When there is a risk of violence, it may also be advisable to find a safe haven. Most cities have shelters for battered women. If you cannot go to a shelter, stay with someone who will not tell your partner where you are. If face-to-face contact is absolutely necessary, arrange for someone to accompany you and meet in a public place, such as a restaurant or store. Even the most volatile of people rarely react violently in public.

The approach discussed in this book can work well in all but the most serious cases of anger. But if violence of any sort is already occurring, or is a possibility, a legal restraint on the batterer is essential before you can attempt to make other changes.

## ANGER WORKSHEETS

*You may wish to make several photocopies of the following pages while they are still blank, since you may be repeating these exercises several times.*

The first step toward lowering your expectations is to increase your awareness of them. As discussed earlier, our expectations are often very subtle. Even if you are unaware of the ones you hold, they will have a negative impact on your life whenever they are unmet.

The first set of exercises will help you increase your general awareness of such expectations, beginning with spotting those that other people have.

## BECOMING AWARE OF YOUR PARTNER'S ANGER AND EXPECTATIONS

1. Begin by describing the unmet expectations, disappointment, hurt, and anger you have observed in another couple's life. Start with what they became angry about, and trace that anger back to the expectation that you think preceded it. (For example, "When my friend told me she was furious at her boyfriend for working late, causing them to leave late for the beach, I saw how her expectation of leaving promptly at five brought on her anger at her boyfriend.")

_____

_____

_____

The following exercises are designed to sensitize you to the prevalence of your partner's anger as well as to what occurs when his or her expectations of you are not met.

2. Does your partner express anger loudly (yelling) or quietly (pouting, acting spiteful)?

Loudly ☐ Quietly ☐

3. Does your partner direct the anger at you, the children, or others, such as friends?

At me ☐ At the children ☐
At others ☐

4. Describe what follows. Do you become defiant? Snap back? Appease his anger? Do the children argue among themselves? (For example, "Once I started adjusting my life to placate his anger, I wasn't able to stop doing so. But now when I do stop, he gets even angrier.")

_____

_____

_____

5. Describe the costs of this anger on your partner, on you, and on your relationship. (For example, "After he gets angry, he feels bad about what he said, and I feel more distant toward him for a while, and we avoid each other.")

_____

_____

_____

6. How long does it take you to recover from these negative feelings? (For example, "After he blasts me, I dislike him for a few weeks.")

_____

_____

_____

7. This exercise will help you trace the progression of your partner's anger to its outcome of resentment and/or bitterness. Describe how over time your partner's unresolved anger has turned into resentment or bitterness. (For example, "She used to get mad at me over how little I discipline the children. Now she resents me all the time because of it.")

_____

_____

_____

The next exercises are aimed at helping you identify the expectations your partner holds of you, especially those unspoken. You begin by linking the anger to expectations.

8. Check off which words your partner uses when angry at you.

| | | | |
|---|---|---|---|
| You should | ☐ | You could | ☐ |
| You ought to | ☐ | You're supposed to | ☐ |

These words reveal your partner's expectations.

9. Describe the issues being discussed when these words are used angrily. (For example, "She gets angry when I don't spend enough time with her and the children or go to social events with her.")

_____

_____

_____

10. List the expectations that give rise to this anger; make the best guess you can if you are unsure. (For example, "She expects me to spend time with the family and to go out with her.")

_____

_____

_____

11. Describe how your partner attempts to get you to meet these expectations. (For example, "Whenever my wife expects something of me, she'll nag, criticize, and ridicule me incessantly, trying to get me to do what she expects.")

_____

_____

_____

As you have probably discovered from these exercises, though unaware and unspoken, expectations can exert an intensely negative influence both on your partner and your relationship. Use any future angry or critical outbursts to help you fill in the blanks you have left above.

## BECOMING AWARE OF YOUR OWN ANGER AND EXPECTATIONS

This set of exercises will help you focus first on the impact *your* anger is having on *your* life and relationship, and second on the expectations underlying your anger.

1. Describe the physiological signs that indicate you are getting angry, especially the inconspicuous ones. (For example, "My stomach churns. I get a headache. My voice gets louder.")

_____

_____

_____

2. Note whether you express that anger loudly, for example, by ridiculing whatever your partner does, or quietly, for example, by spending money you can't afford to spend.

Loudly                    ☐        Quietly                    ☐

3. Describe how you express it. (For example, "When I'm angry at her, I sleep in the spare bedroom.")

_____

_____

_____

4. At whom do you direct your anger? Please check:

Partner  ☐      Friends  ☐      Children  ☐      Other(s)
(For example, colleagues)

_____

_____

5. Describe your partner's reaction to your anger. (For example, does he retaliate? Act defiant? Appease your anger?)

_____

_____

_____

6. We live in a climate that emphasizes venting anger, while ignoring the resulting destructive consequences. The purpose of this exercise is to help sensitize you to the many consequences of anger. Describe the costs of venting your anger in the following areas:

On you. (For example, "I'm always exhausted.")

_____

_____

On your relationship. (For example, "I'm so angry I argue over issues that aren't even important to me.")

_____

_____

On your self-control. (For example, "I seem to be less and less able to control what I say and do.")

_____

_____

On your self-esteem. (For example, "I feel like mud after one of these outbursts.")

_____

_____

On your happiness. (For example, "I'm rarely happy any more. I can't be, because I feel too much resentment.")

_____

_____

On your way of communicating with your partner. (For example, "Whenever I'm angry, everything I say is laced with sarcasm.")

_____

_____

On your problem-solving ability. (For example, "When I'm angry, I'm not interested in resolving anything. All I want to do is blame someone for how bad I feel.")

_____

_____

7. Describe the discomfort you feel when you *don't* vent your anger. (For example, "I feel very anxious until it comes out.")

_____

_____

_____

8. If your motivation for changing your own behavior disappeared after you vented your anger, describe what happens. (For example, "After I've released my anger, I have no strength left to be on my guard in the future against his lying to me, so I fall for it every time.")

_____

_____

_____

9. The following exercise is to help you identify the unfulfilled expectations that are giving rise to your own anger. In the left-hand column below, describe recent incidents in which you have become angry. In the right-hand column, list the expectations you believe gave rise to the anger.

| Incidents you are angry about | Related expectations |
|---|---|
| (For example, "I got angry when my husband refused to go to dinner with me.") | (For example, "I expected him to care enough about me to want to spend some time with me.") |

This is not an exercise most people can do immediately. As angry incidents occur, fill in the chart. If you are having difficulties figuring out your expectations, discuss them with a trusted friend or confidante.

## RESOLVING YOUR ANGER

The next set of exercises is designed to help you decrease the reactive anger you feel by lowering your expectations.

1. Pick one expectation among those you listed above. Describe what it feels like when you think your partner will never do what you expect. (For example, "When I think he doesn't care enough about me to out to dinner with me again, I feel horrible.")

_____

_____

_____

2. Whenever we lower or give up an expectation, especially an unfulfilled one, we grieve over the loss of what we had anticipated, and experience a letdown. Check off which of the following you felt when you lowered your expectation.

| | | | |
|---|---|---|---|
| Angry | ☐ | Confused | ☐ |
| Lonely/empty | ☐ | As if I've failed | ☐ |
| Hopeless/helpless | ☐ | Uncared for | ☐ |

Other(s)

_____

_____

_____

3 Describe those feelings here. (For example, "I feel so empty inside when I think that he will not show he cares about me any more.")

_____

_____

_____

4. List here the people you can talk to about these feelings so that you can become more comfortable with them.

_____

_____

_____

Please note: If you are feeling overwhelmed by these feelings, please discontinue these efforts and discuss them with a counselor first before you relive them here.

5. Lowering your expectations will bring you new insights. Describe any new insights you have had. (For example, "I realized I was much more dependent on my partner than I thought I was.")

_____

_____

_____

6. If your above expectations remain unmet, describe any changes in your life you will need to face and cope with. (For example, "I will have to accept being more alone in my life and find some ways to deal with this.")

_____

_____

_____

## COPING WITH YOUR PARTNER'S ANGER

Please note: If physical violence or the potential of violence is a possibility, *do not attempt the following exercises.* Instead, seek professional help for this serious issue. (Call the police if you feel you are (or may be) in immediate danger, or talk to a therapist about long-term solutions.)

Appeasement is possibly the most common way of handling someone else's anger. If you are attempting to appease your partner's anger, the following set of exercises is geared toward helping you stop.

1. Describe at least one topic that arouses your partner's anger, and say how you try to appease it. (For example, "Whenever my girlfriend gets on the subject of how little money I make, I act overly nice to her to avoid setting her off more.")

_____

_____

_____

2. Define your true "I" position and what you would truly prefer to say and do about this issue, rather than placating your partner. (For example, "Instead of going out of my way to be nice, I'd rather be able to just carry

on like I've done nothing wrong, because I haven't. I know I work hard and earn what I can.")

———————————————————————————————

———————————————————————————————

———————————————————————————————

3. Describe clearly how you will keep from appeasing your partner the next time this incident occurs. (For example, "I will not go out of my way to be overly nice as if I'm guilty of something. Instead, I will continue to do what I had planned to do before she got angry.")

———————————————————————————————

———————————————————————————————

———————————————————————————————

4. As explained earlier, because this is a change on your part, your partner will most likely become reactively angry in response to your *non*appeasement. The more you can anticipate and prepare for this, the better you will be able to handle it. Describe how your partner is likely to react. (For example, "He will probably snap at me about dinner not being ready yet.")

———————————————————————————————

———————————————————————————————

———————————————————————————————

5. Describe how you will avoid appeasing. (For example, "Instead of justifying myself by listing what I've done all day, I will simply say I only just found time to start preparing it.")

———————————————————————————————

———————————————————————————————

———————————————————————————————

6. Once again, it is important to put physical distance between you and your partner if you feel yourself becoming reactive in response to any attacks. Describe here how you will create that distance. (For example, "When I hear my own voice rising, I will get in the car and go for a long drive.")

_____

_____

_____

7. You may find yourself becoming reactive before disengaging or you may simply be unable to disengage because, for example, you're in the middle of feeding your children. If you do become reactive, it is important to drain the emotions off in some way. Describe how you will do so. (For example, "I will get lost in my favorite book, or call up my best friend, or go visit my mother.")

_____

_____

_____

At this point, you've taken a giant step! Now you can deal a little differently with your chronic anger and the issues that give rise to it. However, keep in mind this will be an ongoing process and that you will need to keep reapplying yourself.

# CHAPTER 8

# Pursuit and Distance Between Partners

If you have tried but have had limited success with the approaches suggested so far, if your partner is a master of elusiveness and will not discuss or deal with issues under any circumstances, or if your partner avoids closeness and intimacy in spite of all your efforts, your relationship might be one of pursuit and distance. This dynamic overshadows everything else that occurs in a relationship.

If, after reading this chapter, you find that pursuit and distance is not an issue in your relationship, then consider yourself a fortunate person. Go back and try again to make the changes described earlier. However, pursuit and distance between partners in a relationship is a common phenomenon that may be affecting your attempts to make changes.

A distraught man sat in my office, having agreed to counseling in order to placate his wife. He had been exceedingly distressed ever since she had walked out on him four weeks earlier. Missing her terribly and desperate to get her back, he, for the first time in his married life, was reluctantly acknowledging that there might be some validity to her complaints. But, as he carefully explained to me, he actually felt that he was the victim of her problems. She was always trying to get into his head, overdid this "togetherness thing," and was so emotional and moody, he said. In addition, she seemed to put the children, her family, and even the house before him. His wife was what is known as a pursuer, as will become clearer as you read this chapter.

Her own ongoing sessions with me had given me a very different perspective on their marital problems. During the past five years of their ten-year marriage, she had left him three times. The reasons for each of these separations were the same: he spent most of his time at work or in front of the TV, rarely shared what he was thinking or feeling, and never openly demonstrated any caring for her, and she was totally exhausted from doing all domestic chores, taking care of the children, and trying to make her marriage work. Only when she was thoroughly fed up and wanted nothing further to do with him would he be willing to work on their relationship. But as soon as she became reinvolved with him, he lost interest and became cold, distant, and irresponsible again. He is what is known as a distancer.

## Understanding Pursuit and Distance

There is more truth in the old saying that opposites attract than we may realize. More often than not, people with distinctly opposite personality traits do become emotionally involved. On the surface, at least, they act very differently. One of them, often the woman, tends to be a "people-person." She copes with her insecurity by seeking affirmation through relationships with others—living for, through, or as an extension of the people around her. For this person, togetherness is so desirable that it is sought at the expense of most, if not all, personal autonomy and individuality. She feels emotionally secure (although not truly happy) only when her life revolves around others, and when it does not, she feels useless and worthless. This person is profoundly sensitive, and her emotional reactions are raw and immediate. In addition, she has an intense desire to share her feelings and demands the same from others close to her. Believing the most direct approach to relationship problems is always the best, she is impatient for change, wanting it to take place yesterday.

These traits are often contrasted in a partner who has the opposite characteristics to the same degree. Deep within he too feels insecure, worthless, and lonely. However, instead of overemphasizing relationships and togetherness, he adapts by outwardly stressing his individuality, always wanting to do things his way and to be the center of attention. Unlike the pursuer, he enjoys togetherness only occasionally, and only when he has initiated it. While the pursuer wants to be emotionally close to people, the distancer feels crowded when others come too close. He preserves his own "space" by keeping his thoughts and feelings to himself, making it extremely difficult for his partner to know what he thinks or feels. When he does share something, it is based on his logical thinking rather than on what he feels. Solutions that come from others are viewed with skepticism and hostility, and are usually rejected. Relationship issues and problems are approached indirectly, deferred until the last possible minute, or ignored altogether. Rejecting help from others, he avoids counseling or accomplishes little if he goes. Relationships and people are secondary in importance, while his opinions and possessions, including a partner (who is objectified), are what matter most.

In my experience, about eighty percent of pursuers are women and eighty percent of distancers are men. Put these two distinctly different personality types together in a relationship and an interesting pattern unfolds. Initially, and when things between them are calm and untroubled, one balances the other emotionally. While he is thinking-oriented, she is feeling-oriented. Her directness in dealing with relationship issues is counterbalanced by his avoidance. His desire to be at the center of attention fits well with her desire to make someone else the focus of her attention. It appears to be "oneness" at its best. However, as soon as some stress is added to their relationship, this balance is upset, and what attracted each to the other now becomes a problem. Her overemphasis on how she feels is at odds with his, on what he thinks. His extreme avoidance and procrastination combined with his rigidly logical approach to problem-solving is contrasted by her impatience and impulsivity. She emotionally pursues him by wanting to know what he feels, wanting resolution of their problem, and wanting it at once. Concurrently, he distances himself emotionally from her, seeking "space to think about it," hoping the problem will go away by itself or that she will wait until he comes up with a solution in his own time and way. Frustrated by his indirectness and avoidance, she pursues him harder still, whereupon he feels more crowded and so distances himself still further.

Like a carefully choreographed dance, for every step she takes toward him, he moves one away from her. Or, if he initiates the dance by distancing more, she pursues him. She never "catches" him and he never finds the "space" he seeks, but their stressful dance continues.

### What Motivates Pursuers and Distancers

Driving one person's unceasing pursuit is the hope of catching the distancing partner in order to feel adequate and empowered. With every failed effort, this person believes the goal of self-worth and happiness through togetherness was not achieved because the pursuit was not sufficiently strong. So she redoubles her efforts rather than changing her approach. This usually means giving more and getting less from the relationship and feeling increasingly responsible for its salvation and growth. To accomplish this, she may sacrifice her interests, friends, and remaining emotional autonomy, in the hope that this will finally engage her distancing partner and lead to true intimacy, "completeness," and happiness.

Driving the other's relentless distancing is the deluded belief that the all-important individuality can be preserved while maintaining a relationship in which little is invested emotionally. This partner continues to distance rather than change his approach, at the same time becoming more recalcitrant and negative, and retreating further into what becomes a love affair with himself. Taking less responsibility in and for the relationship, he shares little of what he feels and becomes increasingly preoccupied with his opinions, objects, and his self-importance.

Unable to involve her distancing partner, the pursuer suffers from the accumulating fatigue, disappointment, hurt, and resentment. When she eventually reaches the point of complete exhaustion, and feels unable to "give" any more, she stops her pursuit and distances from her partner in a hurt, angry way, wanting nothing further to do with him. However, when he is no longer being pursued, his need for distancing is removed, and the insecurity he has kept well hidden surfaces. Suddenly he feels worthless, empty, and lonely. In response to these feelings, he begins to pursue her. He tells her he understands what she has been saying all this time, assures her of changes he will make, and apologizes for his past treatment of her. Now, he wants closeness and togetherness. He can't seem to be without it. The pursuer, receiving what she has craved all this time after having felt even more lonely, empty, and worthless while not pursuing, stops her own distancing and becomes intimately involved again. Unfortunately, however, she does so the only way she knows: through pursuit. As soon as this happens, her partner no longer feels lonely and empty, his motivation for changing disappears, and he starts distancing himself again.

## When Distancing and Pursuing Fail

Unwaveringly focused on their partner, pursuers and distancers each perceive themselves as innocent victims of the other's problems, insecurities, or immaturity. This perception causes the entire cycle to be repeated over and over. With every repetition, a little more of the caring for their partner is lost, to be replaced with a growing wall of hurt, disappointment, and loneliness. Again, feeling lonely, and unloved, the pursuer starts looking for other ways to fill the emptiness. Perhaps she becomes overly involved with the children and begins to live for, through, or as an extension of them. Desperately wanting to feel cared about by someone, perhaps she begins an affair. Or, seeking approval from others, she becomes preoccupied with how the house looks or with accumulating money or possessions. At the same time, the distancer's self-centeredness and isolation lead to extreme boredom and emptiness. He, too, begins seeking ways to relieve his discomfort. He may become overly involved with work or try to accumulate money and possessions, which provide a sense of power and control. He may start an affair, which provides a sense of conquest; start overusing alcohol, which relieves the loneliness; or become preoccupied with television or other hobbies and activities, which provide distraction from his growing isolation.

As this pattern between them continues, the pursuer, in time, becomes increasingly weary, frustrated, and overwhelmed with resentment, feeling she has nothing left but the chase. The solution has become the problem. Hoping to put off failure just a little longer, she tries harder than ever to change her partner. To accomplish this, she ceaselessly tries to involve him by manipulating, controlling, intimidating, or trying to ensnare him. And she sincerely believes that she is doing these things for her partner's own good. For the distancer, the struggle to stay elusive and uncommitted becomes a challenge, and he cannot acknowledge any responsibility for what is occurring or admit that his distancing has not helped. And most of all, he cannot admit he has failed. So he continues to distance from his partner without questioning why or asking himself what he is running from. Like his partner, he is trying to put off dealing with the inevitable a little longer.

The consequences of these mutual deceptions finally take their toll. Emotionally exhausted, drained of much love for one another, and involved in a multitude of distractions (though still lonely), the two partners trudge through their life together as if alone, going through the motions of a relationship but without any real meaning. Or they move on to other relationships. Concluding that her unhappiness was due to her partner's distancing, and not her pursuit, the pursuer also pursues her new partner. She continues to deceive herself, believing that this time she will find someone through whom she can feel secure, fulfilled, and loved. Concluding that his unhappiness was due to his partner's pursuit, and not his distancing, the distancer also distances from his new partner. He deceives himself that this time he will have a close and loving relationship with little effort, resposibility or involvement on his part.

## Recognizing Pursuers and Distancers

As described in chapter 5 on balancing "I" and "we," in any relationship there is a continual struggle between the participants' desires for individuality and togetherness. The wish for individuality is represented in each person's struggle to be "me", while the pull toward togetherness is seen in the struggle to be a part of "we." The ideal is to achieve a balance between the ability to be part of "we" without giving up too much of "me." Since only a thin line separates the two, it is easy to err in one direction or the other. When we seek too much "I", we overemphasize our individuality at the expense of the relationship and become an over-sized self. The consequences of this are always negative. As one woman reported, "He always does his thing and never considers me. I'm so sick of it I don't even want to be around him any more." When we overemphasize a relationship at the expense of our individuality, we seek too much "we" and become selfless. This results in such dire consequences as not knowing who we are any more and feeling incomplete and empty without our partner .

Our oversized self fears intimacy and commitment, believing it will be lost or smothered if too close to another person. We use both emotional and physical distance from others to preserve our fragile individuality. On the other hand, because we tend to gravitate to our opposites who will make up for our weaknesses or shortcomings, the selfless person always seeks out an oversized self. When someone willing to give up individuality connects emotionally with someone trying to preserve it at all costs, a pursuit and distance relationship develops. However, pursuit and distance are not set traits, and a couple can switch roles in different situations. Men tend to be emotional distancers and sexual pursuers, and women tend to be emotional pursuers and sexual distancers. (See the breakdown of specific traits of pursuers and distancers, on pages 183–188. You might find it interesting to compare your usual traits with this list to see whether you are usually a pursuer or a distancer.) These roles may also change with different people or relationships. A pursuer may encounter a more aggressive pursuer and distance herself from him, and vice versa.

People often ask when the pattern of pursuit and distance begins in a relationship. "It wasn't always like this between us," they say. In my experience, it begins when an emotional or a legal commitment is made to the relationship. Either the pursuer or the distancer can start it. One woman described it thus: "He pursued me until I'd dropped most of my friends and interests and he became central in my life. Then he pulled away, and I haven't been able to catch him since." And one man reported, "Once we got married, she became bent on controlling every part of my life."

Many times it is difficult for pursuers to recognize distancers, because of their chameleonlike behavior. Initially the distancer provides the pursuer with togetherness and intimacy, but then withdraws. As one woman said, "He was the sweetest, most loving person before we got married. Then he changed completely." The pursuer stays in the relationship primarily with the expectation and false hope that the now-distancing partner will change back to what she sees as his real self. The longer this continues, the bigger the gap becomes between her expectation and the way her partner actually behaves. The result is increasing disappointment, hurt, and anger. These draining emotions continue until she acknowledges the gap between her expectations and reality. It is important to realize that in the work or business world, distancers and pursuers frequently behave in a manner completely opposite to the way they behave in a personal relationship. As a pursuer complained, "No one would believe how aloof he is when we close the door at home."

## Understanding How to End Pursuing and Distancing

Both pursuit and distance are reactive behaviors, which, like all old brain behaviors, become progressively worse over time, unless one partner's efforts succeed in putting a stop to them. Hoping that your particular situation will be different next time or is an exception to the rule is to wait for something that will not happen. There are few exceptions. However, on the positive side, you need not continue this dance any longer. With understanding and effort, it can be changed and your situation will improve significantly.

Chapter 1 discussed the fact that in any relationship the motivation for change is rarely equal and that change will be initiated by the person who is most uncomfortable. This is especially relevant for pursuit and distance because the particular characteristics of the pursuer, as compared to those of the distancer, initially make the pursuer more open to change. Pursuers prefer to deal with problems rather than avoid them, and they tend to be open to new ideas rather than resistant to them. They are ready for change and willing to put the necessary effort into it, in contrast to a distancer's willingness to wait, seemingly forever. In addition, the pursuers are the obvious losers in the pursuit-distance dance and are more tired, frustrated, and unhappy than the distancer (or, at least, more aware of being unhappy). As one pursuer said, "He's got it good. I always give up my needs for his." Despite an apparent disregard for the relationship, the distancer has more to lose than the pursuer if things change in their relationship. The distancer will have to give up more if the pursuer's life no longer revolves around him, and he will have to learn to give as well as take.

For these reasons, the pursuer is more motivated to initiate change. A distancer will rarely initiate change and never changes in response to direct efforts by others. He will change only when he fears losing his pursuer, and this can happen only when the pursuer stops her pursuit. Distancers tend to change in direct proportion to how much their pursuers modify their pursuit. Frequently women ask me why they have to do all the changing. And the answer is that it does not always have to be the woman, but it does always have to be the pursuer. Pursuers complain that this isn't fair or reasonable, and I agree. But in my experience, this is nonetheless the way it is and must be dealt with, regardless of whether or not it is right or reasonable. The majority of people I see in my office are pursuers, and at the outset each one believes she is an exception and hopes to succeed in her pursuit. But ultimately, every one of them is disappointed. One pursuer summed it up like this:

> I kept thinking that if I were a nice enough person—never purposely hurt anyone and helped everyone I could—things would get better. I would be rewarded in spite of my shortcomings. I found out after years of disappointment that how good a person is doesn't matter, and I still have to change my behavior.

A pursuer involved in an ongoing pursuit and distance relationship has three options: to continue the pursuit, to separate, or to
stop pursuing. The first option of continuing to pursue the distancer with the hope of some day emotionally engaging him is the
substance of every pursuer's fantasy. But it remains a fantasy, which
ultimately leads to frustration, exhaustion, and emotional bank-
ruptcy. Separation is dealt with in chapter 10. This leaves the third
option to discuss here. If a pursuer is fearful of ending the relationship despite wishing to do so or is undecided about ending it, the
best approach is to put the decision on hold and concentrate on
learning how to stop the pursuit. (She can still decide to leave her
partner at a later date, if all else fails.) Before reading any further,
each pursuer needs to look honestly at her own life and ask: "With
all the time and effort I've already put in, has my approach of pursuit accomplished its purpose? Or are stress, resentment, and failure
all I have to show for my efforts? How much more am I willing to
take? How much *can* I take?" If, after all your pursuing, you are no
closer to your goal of togetherness, yet you do not want to end your
relationship, your only remaining course is to stop pursuing.

Pursuers may consider themselves superior to or more fault-free
than their distancing partners and think they do not need to change.
Or they may not understand what they need to change. Their pursuit prevents them from recognizing their own shortcomings,
which include some of the following characteristics.

Pursuers are dependent on togetherness. They *need* it like addicts
need a fix. Without someone to live for or through, pursuers feel incomplete and depressed. This dependency leads to an obsession
with the distancing partner and the need to stay in a relationship—
even a bad one.

Because pursuers' need for love is so great, they end up settling
for very little in relationships. However, their unaddressed needs
and unmet expectations produce an inordinate amount of disappointment, frustration, and anger, which is expressed in hostile,
critical ways. On the other hand, pursuers tend to be naive and
overly trusting, which often results in self-imposed victimization.

At the same time, pursuers are overly responsible people. They assume responsibility for everyone else's problems and think that only they can solve those problems. They don't believe other people have the ability to run their own lives. This kind of caretaking ends up being manipulative and controlling, and their attempt to control those around them prevents the very closeness pursuers seek, as people resist the efforts to change them. Many pursuers who are frustrated in the pursuit of their partner turn to their children and become overinvolved in their lives. This doesn't solve the problems in the relationship and can create worse problems for the children later on.

When pursuers talk about how much work a relationship takes, they don't really comprehend the degree of work required on their part. They talk about wanting to change, but are easily discouraged when faced with obstacles and find it difficult to follow through on their goals. They find it easy to blame others, and their intense emotionality and reactivity means they repeatedly provoke emotional crises in the relationship. They continually try to pressure, control, or rescue their partners, and to vent their own frustrations. Even those who eventually leave their present relationship find that they repeat the same patterns in their subsequent relationships, which helps to destroy them too.

Distancers are not the independent people they profess to be. Without the pursuer chasing them, distancers can no longer focus their efforts on moving away from pursuers, and their illusion of autonomy disappears. What happens after this point will be determined by how much the distancer genuinely cares for his partner and not by what he says or appears to feel. When the pursuit stops, even if the pursuers does absolutely nothing more, the distancer's comfortable and complacent world is shaken up, providing an opportunity for real change. Once this is provided, the next move is up to the distancer. Pursuers only have to make the first changes, not all the changes. But the only way the pursuer can reach the distancer is by distancing herself from him—emotionally and physically.

You may ask, "What good is it if I have to get distant from my partner to get him back? I want more togetherness, not less!" But you need to look at this nonpursuit in an overall context, remembering that it will be a temporary rather than permanent condition.

It also provides you with an opportunity to work on your own shortcomings. Remember, too, that stopping your pursuit will leave you no worse off than you were to begin with. If you are a pursuer, you have not had a relationship of substance with your distancing partner for a long time. All you have had is a glimmer of false hope that some day you may engage him in a meaningful relationship. Halting your pursuit allows you to get on with your life with, or without, your distancing partner. In other words, you really have nothing to lose, because trying to directly change a distancer is always futile. A common mistake made by pursuers is becoming obsessed with getting their partner to change or to go to a counselor. Distancers *can* change, but only in response to the pursuer's changes.

A woman of forty-seven spoke about her husband who attends counseling but has not changed as she had hoped he would: he still stays out late, overspends, and lies to her. She is totally drained from arguing, pressuring, demanding, and giving him ultimatums. They have finally separated over these issues. In her own words, "I've become a bitter, unhappy, and depressed nag, and have wasted eleven years of my life." This is the typical outcome for a pursuer who waits for a distancer to change, or to reciprocate, or approve of her changes. It is an inescapable journey into despair and emptiness, since the change either never happens or happens only after it is too late. When, occasionally, the pursuer's pressure does keep the distancer "in line," it happens at an enormous cost to the pursuer. One wife described this vividly: "If I pressure, nag, manipulate, and get angry enough at him, he shapes up for a time, but it leaves me exhausted and consumed with hate." As is natural, all pursuers look for a pain-free road out of their predicament, but it doesn't exist. Either they continue their fruitless pursuit or they stop, and both are painful. Their only choice is whether or not to put their pain to constructive use. In reality, the only way to catch a distancer (if he can be caught) is to outdistance him by being more distant than he is. And for a pursuer, that's a living hell.

The next chapter and the worksheets that follow it will help pursuers end this painful cycle.

## Traits of Distancers and Pursuers

The following lists of traits are commonly found in pursuers and distancers. Sometimes a few of the traits are reversed. For instance, a pursuer may be impatient, overresponsible, and a people-person, which is typical of pursuers, but instead of being open and expressive with her feelings, she is closed and noncommunicative, which is atypical of pursuers. Or a distancer may be irresponsible and unsociable, typical traits, but open and communicative about feelings, characteristics atypical of distancers. All the traits listed below might be reversed in this way. In some people, the traits fit only partially or occasionally.

The number of these traits you have, and to what degree, will help reveal whether you are a pursuer or a distancer, and thus involved in a pursuit/distance relationship. If, after reviewing these traits, you believe that few of them apply to you or your relationship or apply so mildly that they cause few problems, then, for all practical purposes, you are not involved in a pursuit/distance relationship.

## Emotional Distancers

(Predominantly male)

SEXUAL STYLE: Pursuit.
SENSE OF SELF: On the surface, aggrandized self; strongly individualistic. In reality, pseudo-individualistic. Individualistic only in a supportive environment, such as at home, in presence of, but unresponsive to, his partner.
Does things in own way, through defiance or passive resistance.
A leader and self-initiator.
Sees the world as centered on himself. Tries to be the center of attention. Feels unappreciated.
Overly self-concerned and self-protective; always looking out for self. Difficulty perceiving others' points of view.
Prefers independent activities with "buddies," not organized group activities. Chooses to be different for its own sake.

Experiences his individuality to the exclusion of relationship.

TRUST: Highly suspicious of others and relationships with them. Pessimist about others' motives.

EMOTIONS: Primarily object-oriented. Relates to and puts material things first, feelings and people second. Results in an overemphasis on thinking and logic.

Fears emotions and emotionality. Avoids them.

Unemotional, and affect is elusive. Impossible to tell his feelings by looking at or listening to him.

Only emotion expressed regularly is anger. Either explosively and briefly or passive-aggressively, as if he's not angry when he really is. Self-gratifying and unresponsive. Little sympathy for, or empathy with, others. Feels little for others or self.

EMOTIONAL BOUNDARIES: Overprotected. Needs a lot of "space."

RELATIONSHIP SKILLS: Lacking.

SENSE OF RESPONSIBILITY: Underresponsible; feels little responsibility for his situation or relationship. Tends to blame others.

Most comfortable emotionally (although not truly happy) behaving like a "baby."

CAPACITY TO CHANGE: Lacks insight and/or follow-through.

Inability to adjust. Clings rigidly to position regardless of circumstances.

Resists direct change. Tends to evolve rather than changing directly in response to circumstances. Will change when faced with loss of significant other.

Rejects advice, counseling. Solutions must come from self. Frustrates others' efforts to change him.

RHYTHM OF INITIATING CHANGE: Tends to be overly "patient." Procrastinates. Avoids facing relationship problems. Prone to relationship paralysis.

PATTERN OF EMOTIONS: Little variation. Tends to be reasonable, but boring. Depends on his pursuer for highs and lows.

RELATIONSHIP EXPECTATIONS: Expects the pursuer to always be there. Prone to despair and self-pity when not fulfilled.

PERSONAL PROBLEM-SOLVING STYLE: Avoidance. Seeks peace, avoids emotional crises. Believes if you ignore a problem long enough, it will go away.

CONTROL AND MANIPULATION: Strives to maintain central position to protect self from getting hurt.

Manipulates environment to meet his needs.

DECISION MAKING: Decisions made and then clung to regardless of changes in circumstances.

VIEW OF LOVE: Overemphasizes practical aspects. Minimal expression of love, sharing, or romance, except when courting or pursuing a distancing partner.

TYPICAL BELIEF: Love is fine, but it doesn't pay the bills.

SEXUALITY: Physical enjoyment takes precedence over caring. Sex seen as conquest or performance, not shared experience. Objectifies partner.

SUBSTITUTE ACTIVITIES: Overly involved with objects, e.g., sports, cars, house (for prestige), work, sexual liaisons (conquest), alcohol.

SELF-DECEPTION: Believes overemphasis on individuality brings a sense of security, self-esteem, contentment. Fears emotional closeness. Believes he can evade a pursuer.

DEMEANOR: In later years: boring to be involved with. Arrogant, cynical, pessimistic, negative. Prone to self-pity.

FACIAL CHARACTERISTICS AFTER FORTY: Appears emotionless. Dark circles under eyes.

GREATEST RELATIONSHIP DIFFICUTLTY: Denial of problem. Avoidance of relationship issues.

TYPICAL STATEMENTS: "I like myself the way I am and you should too. If you don't like me the way I am, you're free to leave. I give you a comfortable life, don't sleep around—what more do you want?"

# Emotional Pursuers

(Predominantly female)

SEXUAL STYLE: Distance.

SENSE OF SELF: Strongly nonindividualistic. Has difficulty being alone or acting independently for any length of time.

Rarely does things on own. Primarily does what others want. Tends to be clinging and overly anxious.

A follower. Depends on others for guidance.

Sees the world as centered on others. "Gives to get." Feels taken for granted.

Overly concerned and protective of others. Always looking out for others, never for self.

Overly adaptive. Chooses to be like others or to yield for the sake of unity.

Feels empty without interaction with others. Constantly seeking love, approval, and appreciation. Will give up individuality for the sake of relationship.

TRUST:  Tends to be naive about relationships. Optimist about others' motives.

Overly trusting; frequently taken advantage of.

EMOTIONS:  Primarily people- and feeling-oriented. Places these above material things.

Seeks out emotions and emotionality.

Overemotional, and affect is heightened. Openly shows feelings to everyone.

Expresses a full range of emotions. Frequently intensely expressive, at the expense of thought or reason.

Overinvolved in others. A "co-dependent." Overly sympathetic and empathetic. Heightened response to others. Avoids pain. Tries to protect others from consequences of their behavior.

EMOTIONAL BOUNDARIES:  Ill-defined. May be nosy, intrusive ("always has to know what's going on with everyone in the family at all times").

RELATIONSHIP SKILLS:  Immaturely applied.

SENSE OF RESPONSIBILITY:  Overly responsible. Assumes too much responsibility for the relationship. Assumes solution is in her power with sufficient effort.

Most comfortable emotionally (although not truly happy) when tending to the needs of others. Tends to infantilize others.

Is a "rescuer."

CAPACITY TO CHANGE:  Insight into others, but little into self. Often held back by looking for explanations. Much talk of change, while still passive.

Changes made to appease. Avoids significant change because of anticipated pain and lack of approval. Wants prior guarantees.

Open to direct change. Overly amenable. Fears taking a stand and dealing with consequences. Believes problems must be dealt with instantly.

Seeks advice, counseling. Open to offered solutions via own efforts.

RHYTHM OF INITIATING CHANGE: Overly impatient. Cannot delay dealing with problems. Lacks restraint; impulsive.

PATTERN OF EMOTIONS: High peaks and deep lows. Depends on the distancer for stability.

RELATIONSHIP EXPECTATIONS: High expectations of others, low for self. Believes she expects "nothing in return," but holds expectations no one could fulfill. Prone to resentment, bitterness in later years. Very critical of others.

PERSONAL PROBLEM-SOLVING STYLE: Emotional engagement. Seeks emotionally charged, reactive situations. Uncomfortable in calm situations. Tends to provoke reactivity and crises. Generates worry about everyone and everything.

CONTROL AND MANIPULATION: Controls to protect others from themselves.

Manipulates, controls others through guilt, advice, retaliation, criticism, and/or submissiveness. Acts for others "own good."

Feels powerless and ultimately incapable. Seeks someone to exert control for and over her.

DECISION MAKING: Difficult, confused, inconsistent. Depends on others to make decisions (parents, partner).

VIEW OF LOVE: Overly romantic. Overlooks practical aspects of relationship.

TYPICAL BELIEF: Love conquers all.

SEXUALITY: Caring for the partner takes precedence over physical enjoyment. Sex seen as a sign of caring for and by partner.

SUBSTITUTE ACTIVITIES: Overly involved with family, house (for approval), sexual liaisons (to feel cared for), medications, particularly tranquilizers.

SELF-DECEPTION: Believes living for or as extension of partner brings a sense of security, self-esteem, contentment. Believes can catch a distancer.

DEMEANOR: Assumed invulnerability. Self-righteous. In later years: bitter, cold, emotionally and physically fatigued. Prone to martyrdom.

FACIAL CHARACTERISTICS AFTER FORTY: Stress lines (from turmoil, anger). Fatigued look (from pursuit).

GREATEST RELATIONSHIP DIFFICULTY: Inability to remain uninvolved, particularly with own children.

TYPICAL STATEMENTS: "All I ever needed was a home and to be loved. I'll do whatever I have to do to keep everyone happy. If he really cared about me, he would just know what I want."

# CHAPTER 9

# *Stopping Pursuit:*
## Guidance for Pursuers

At this point, if you identify yourself as a distancer, the most productive thing you can do is give this book to the pursuer in your life, who is the one most likely to initiate the necessary changes. If you have identified yourself as a pursuer and want to improve your situation, all you need to do is *never pursue a distancer.* However, following this guiding rule is not easy for pursuers. Below are some specific ways you can avoid pursuing your partner.

In the emotional sphere, don't initiate conversation or give advice (and even if asked for advice, refrain from giving it). Abstain from trying to change or improve your partner in any way. Do not seek his emotional support or help with any of your problems, concerns, or worries. Do not look to him as someone to talk to. If you have children, you have probably been raising them nearly single-handedly anyway, so you know you can continue to manage without his input on a short-term basis. If you have been babying him, stop. Identify whatever you are doing for him, and stop doing it. For example, stop doing his laundry, picking up after him, cooking specially for him, or waiting on or for him. Stop "keeping the peace." If you have been intervening between him and others, be it children, family, or friends, stop doing so. However, if there is any risk of physical abuse of the children, you must intervene and also seek help for this problem.

On the physical level, do not initiate expressions of affection, such as hugging, kissing, and saying "I love you," or "I'll miss you," or asking questions such as "Do you love me?". And do not appease your partner sexually any longer. If you truly do not want to have sex with him, then don't. Socially, do not plan your schedule around his, and do not do things with him. This is not the time for a romantic vacation or a second honeymoon. If he spends his spare time at home, arrange to be out while he is there. Do things with friends or family or by yourself. In short, do as little as possible for him or with him, with the goal of doing absolutely nothing.

Whatever you do, *do not give your distancing partner this book to read*. Though you may be dying to share these new insights with him, he would not act on them even if he did read this book (which is unlikely if you suggest it). More important, you will be revealing your plans, giving him more resolve to resist your changes. Changing your own behavior is hard enough without being baited by such remarks as "I know what you're doing—you're just following the advice in that book!" or, even worse, having your efforts undermined.

### Learning to Change Your Behavior

Stopping pursuit, as described here, doesn't have to be done gracefully. Few people enjoy it. Most are quite angry about having to do it. But nothing will change for the pursuer until it is done. The point is to do it *for* yourself, not to punish the distancer.

You will need to learn how to fill your life in new ways, seeking other people who will meet your emotional "needs". You may have to work at meeting new people. This would be a great time to take a class or develop a long-forgotten interest. After so many years of focusing on your partner's interests, you may find it difficult to remember what you used to enjoy, but try! Given a little time and thought, it will all come back to you. You must also learn to deal with the lack of physical affection, satisfaction, and pleasure. (Of course, this is not the time to find a lover.) Since pursuers tend to carry togetherness to an extreme, you will be forced to develop emotional autonomy. Though it takes a while to do so, once you have made a start, it will grow and you will begin to enjoy it.

During this period it will be essential that you deal with unrealistic expectations and the fantasy of some day catching your partner through pursuit. Most pursuers are expert at avoiding self-change, and tend to blame everyone else for their unhappiness. Thus, in addition to giving up your pursuit, you need to change your expectations. Otherwise, pulling back from your partner will merely become another manipulation intended to change your mate. The real improvement for a pursuer comes from reevaluation of, and change within, herself. The combination of lowering your expectations (as discussed in chapter 7) and giving up your pursuit will cause this to occur.

A pursuer's improvement can occur only after her illusion of finding happiness and completeness through someone else collapses. Though this is painful, it has to occur. Otherwise, even though she withdraws from her pursuit, she will continue to live in a make-believe world, waiting for her situation to improve without making the inner changes necessary to improve it. These steps are indeed extreme, but drastic measures are called for where pursuit and distance exist in a relationship.

You will wonder how to explain your change of behavior if you are questioned about it. You can do so quite simply and directly by stating your "I" position. You might, for example, say "I'm unhappy with the way our relationship is going and I want to change it." Once again, it will be essential to do so nonreactively, without defending your position or seeking approval. Most important, do not present it in a defiant or attacking manner. The same applies if you are explaining this to your children or other relatives. You no longer need to justify your actions to anyone.

Most pursuers consider stopping their pursuit only at a point of absolute desperation, which usually tends to begin at age thirty or later. Prior to this, pursuers have too much enthusiasm, energy, and false hope to think that their pursuit might fail. Only when the futility of the pursuit begins to become apparent, when they are exhausted and despairing, does the hopelessness of ever achieving their goal be-

come evident. This is when they will begin to question the value of
their unthinking pursuit. Since pursuers are dealing with long-en-
trenched emotional habits, it takes some time to accomplish what is
outlined here. And, typically, initial efforts are met with repeated failures. Here are some stories about such initial failures.

Whenever this wife in her mid-thirties pulled back from pursuing her husband, he offered her assurances of how he would
change, adding how good a person he thought her to be. Because of
these assurances and his "charm," her willpower evaporated. However, when she became involved with him again, he immediately
started distancing himself, and she was left with nothing once more.
After eight months of this back and forth dance, she finally became
strong enough to resist his verbal assurances. Instead, she waited for
a change in his actions.

A male pursuer in his late forties reported how every time he
pulled back from his girlfriend, she would become verbally abusive.
He would then succumb to her pressure. But as soon as he gave up
making any changes and resumed arranging his life to revolve
around hers, she returned to her unresponsive and manipulative behavior. It took this man eighteen months to reach the point where
he was able to resist her intimidation.

A woman in her fifties had to struggle very hard to stop her pursuit, and during this time, her marriage oscillated between repeated
separations and reconciliations. She recalled all her difficulties in
following through with her plans. She was certain that her husband
would retaliate by withholding money; it took her a year to develop
the emotional, social, and financial resources to act. She cut down
the number of things she did for him, responded sexually only
when it suited her, and stopped placating his temper. She also developed the strength to face her greatest fear, that of being unloved.

The pursuer's emotional make-up makes it very difficult for her
to stop pursuing her partner. Often, she wants a guarantee of success before she undertakes any changes but, unfortunately, there can
be no guarantees in life or relationships. It is necessary to do what
we believe we need to do, accepting the risks involved. In addition,
most pursuers want their partners to approve of their changes. But,

in reality, the partners always react with initial disapproval and often with retaliation, as well. Since pursuers tend to be followers, they look to their distancing partners to initiate change, yet distancers will always put off resolving their relationship problems. Thus it is emotionally fatal to follow a distancer's lead. In addition, most pursuers find it extremely difficult to face the idea of being alone. This is clearly described in the following confession: "My own insecurity keeps me from following through. Not so much the fear of losing *him,* but the fear of being alone, of having to admit to myself that I've failed to keep us together. I'm not ready to face that yet."

The first and most important step for the pursuer is to be willing to make changes by taking action, not just talking about it. When pursuers reach this point, they have arrived at the beginning of a significant, and ultimately tremendous, life improvement.

## Emotions Pursuers Will Experience Before They Succeed

Developing a sense of identity independent of their partners usually causes pursuers extreme discomfort. Thus, as they pull back from the object of their pursuit, they experience a painful loss. The initial reaction to this loss is usually either temporary relief or a feeling of anger and betrayal. Then a sense of nothingness will surface, and the pursuer will feel confused, empty, unloved, unwanted, incapable, lonely, and incomplete. If these feelings don't appear, it means the pursuer has not disengaged enough but is still pursuing. True grieving over this loss will usher in a period of profound self-evaluation, accompanied by a variety of painful emotions. Pursuers will feel guilty, cheated, confused, angry, and hurt. They will worry that they are becoming selfish, that they have failed, that they have permanently alienated their partner, that they will lose him, and will suffer loneliness forever. This fear is not unrealistic as there can be no guarantees in relationships. However, if a pursuer actually does "lose" her partner, this can't be seen as a true loss since she did not "have" him to begin with, and the potential for separation was already high.

The degree of pain a pursuer will feel will be proportionate to how extreme a pursuer she is. Being emotionally oriented, she will feel unnatural and awkward when not pursuing. She will feel untrue to herself because of the perception that she is not expressing or following her "real" feelings. This is an unrealistic view of how change happens. Even when we first learn to walk, ride a bicycle, or work at a new job, we experience stress. If we always stayed with what felt right at the moment, we would still be crawling around on our hands and knees, unwilling to take our first step! Nonpursuit will also feel like "game playing" or being manipulative and deceitful. However, nonpursuit is not deceitful; it is a temporary change in behavior for the purpose of freeing the pursuer from exhaustion, frustration, and resentment and increasing her happiness and satisfaction. In reality, pursuing is deceitful—to self and partner.

Few can succeed with the first try, and there will be an inner tug-of-war between the forces for and against pursuit. On one side will be the self-deluding fantasy that pursuit works; on the other side will be the need to initiate change. This struggle will lead to mood swings, where you will first want to give up the effort and then stick with it. One day you may feel hopeless and the next, hopeful again.

During this time, every pursuer will continue to ask herself why she should go through all this. The answer is that while acute pain is inevitable, she does have a choice. She can put the pain she feels to constructive use to improve her life eventually or she can let it drag on for the rest of her life. Any hope that she can avoid this pain is futile. She will never wake up to find that her situation has resolved itself or that her distancing husband has resolved it. In contrast to this, nonpursuit will be an exercise in dealing with reality. This painful period is temporary rather than permanent. No matter how painful the nonpursuit, a pursuer will be better off not pursuing because the changes she makes during this time come from within herself. One pursuer, for example, said that she learned about the joys of dignity and personal autonomy when she stopped her pursuit. Another said, "After four years of our living together with no commitment from him, I'm ready to settle down. If he's not, then I need to end it here and get on with my life."

Though the emptiness you will feel will be terrible, the best thing you can do about it is nothing. It is essential to wait it out rather than to revert to your pursuit. What will grow from the pain of this emptiness is the seed of self-development and personal autonomy instead of dependency. Initially you will feel a lot of anger and hurt, but it will be necessary to transform these feelings in order to put them to constructive use. One of the reasons pursuers have difficulty following through on making changes is that when they release their anger, they temporarily feel better. But they also lose the strength to follow through on making any self-change.

During this difficult time, try to stay focused on refraining from pursuit, rechanneling your pain into overcoming your own shortcomings, and learning how to feel better about yourself. Don't get lost in trying to understand what went wrong or who is to blame. Pursuers have to stop blaming the distancer and focus on changing themselves if their lives are going to improve. But be prepared for the fact that you will frequently feel depressed and sorry for yourself. Keep this depression in perspective, however, since it is a normal reaction in this period and a prerequisite for making positive changes. Ultimately your inner contentment and future happiness will depend on whether or not you develop the fortitude to make it through this difficult time. It will help to accomplish this if you start by taking small doses of this pain, increasing them over time, just like taking increasing doses of something you are allergic to in order to become desensitized to it.

When you are feeling too despairing, you can allow yourself to resume pursuing. Be prepared for a slow and painful process. If you find yourself thinking of suicide as an alternative, stop following this course and seek professional help immediately. Take it at your own pace. Let your body tell you how much it can handle. People usually do this work in spurts. First, they stop pursuing, then more problems develop and they work on them again, and the problems decrease again. There is no predictable length of time this work takes; it is often a lifelong process, with the pursuer becoming increasingly stronger and less dependent on her partner and on her children, material possessions, alcohol, or pills for happiness and peace of mind.

This empty, confusing, and painful time may lead you to impulsive behavior, such as provoking arguments, overeating, and overspending. Knowing this in advance can help you resist such impulses. A pursuer already has enough problems in her life without adding new ones. Be prepared to lose sexual desire, which is a common reaction for pursuers because sexual desire and caring for their partner are intertwined and inseparable. (This is less true for distancers who tend to see sex as a physical act unconnected to feelings.)

Though this period may feel like the end, it's really the beginning. It is at this point that a pursuer changes from a clinging, anxious, dependent, and needy approval-seeker to a more autonomous, calm, self-assured adult. One woman reported later: "I got a job, went back to school, went on a diet, started speaking up and not putting up with his garbage any longer. I feel so much stronger."

## Dealing with a Distancer's Opposition to Nonpursuit

In addition to learning how to deal with the changes to them brought on by their nonpursuit, pursuers will also have to deal with their partner's changes. These, too, will be profound. Under the calm, unemotional, unexpressive, and seemingly distant and uncaring exterior of a distancer is a desperate person. And this desperation is also generated by self-deception—the expectation that the distancer can get more out of a relationship than he puts into it.

The distancer is about to face the cost of that deception, which has been avoided for so long. But first the distancer will mount a no-holds-barred campaign to get the pursuer to pursue again. The stakes are high. If successful, the distancer will not have to change, and can continue to be the focus of the pursuer's attention.

If unsuccessful, the distancer, in the absence of pursuit, will no longer be able to focus on running away from the pursuer, so will begin to experience a deep emptiness. At this point the self-deception begins to crumble. First, as the pursuer pulls back, the distancer usually feels relief, lasting from a few days to several weeks. This is followed by a sense of missing the disengaged partner. If this longing has not begun within two months, the pursuer either has not stopped pursuing completely or has been inconsistent—pursuing one day, not pursuing the next day.

It is also possible that there is no real interest left in the relationship. In my experience, the only way to truly determine how much, if any, caring a distancer has for his pursuing partner is for her to stop pursuing. If he cares for her, after the initial reaction against the nonpursuit, he will start pursuing her. If he does not care enough, he will move on to something or someone else. The question of whether or not their partner cares for them haunts pursuers unceasingly. They may dread finding the answer, which will be evident when the pursuer has successfully stopped pursuing and the distancer doesn't pursue her. It is extremely painful for a pursuer to find out, after all that time, that her partner really doesn't love her after all. However, after the initial shock, it can also be very liberating to finally know the reality and be able to make decisions based on that knowledge.

## The Distancer's "Nice" Phase

While the pursuer is struggling with the consequences of nonpursuit, the distancer must deal with issues of his own. He begins to sense that the apparently comfortable and self-indulgent world he has grown accustomed to is in danger of being lost. Rather than admit defeat at this point and change, he will try to bring the relationship back to its earlier status. This opposition usually goes through the following stages. First, the distancer will become "nice," and his most charming traits will come to the fore. As one pursuer described it, "He's so charming when he's trying to win me back, I feel like I'm under a spell." There are promises and assurances of how he now "sees the error" of his ways, and he says whatever she wants to hear, whatever will seduce her back into pursuing him again. This is frequently a time of suddenly offered gifts and trips after years of neglect.

At this stage, the pursuer's common dilemma is whether or not to believe in the distancer's assurances and become re-involved. She is finally getting what she has wanted for so long that she is tempted to drop her changed behavior and return to her previous ways. The earlier self-deception reappears, while there is also great confusion over whether to trust him again. In addition, she feels guilty about her distrust and fears that she will permanently push her partner away if she does not return to her pursuit. The pursuer usually must struggle with her feelings about how "selfishly," "manipulatively," and "deceitfully" she is behaving. She will usually anguish most over the issue of whether or not her actions are deceptive and manipulative.

I believe that what we consider to be honesty is often distorted by our self-righteousness or self-deception. But when we deceive ourselves in ways which allow us to avoid making difficult changes, we are certainly being dishonest. Viewed in this way, our behavior is better seen as neither right nor wrong, but rather as helpful or unhelpful. For example, a woman who pursued her husband for seventeen years remained "true" and "honest" to herself, but all she had to show for it was an embittered relationship. When she acted "dishonestly" by stopping her pursuit, her marriage and both her and her husband's lives improved.

If a pursuer resumes pursuing, usually her false hopes revive, and she gives up her struggle for autonomy. Then her partner immediately distances again, the old pattern resumes and she becomes unhappy. Since this is bound to happen, it is essential that the pursuer learn from it and look at the mistakes she made. This is the time to use the energy from the resulting anger at the distancer to make the necessary personal changes. The pursuer will have to move past this point, not allowing herself to be seduced by the temporary charms of her distancing partner. A clue that the distancer's "niceness" is only temporary is when the promises are not being carried out. As one woman put it, "He says all the right words, but then he doesn't do anything about them." If a pursuer finds herself in this situation, she can use the anger she feels to strengthen her resolve to be stronger the next time.

### The Distancer's "Ugly" Phase

If being nice has failed to restore the familiar pattern of pursuit and distance, the distancer will become "ugly," though sometimes ugliness comes first, followed by niceness, depending on the distancer's personal style. It is also common to be both, one day (or minute) being charming, the next ugly, then nice again, and so on. This phase puts tremendous pressure on the pursuer. Not only is she dealing with her feelings of confusion, emptiness, and despair, but she must also deal with the distancer's various forms of opposition. For example, in his desperation to avoid looking within himself, the distancer may blame everyone else for what is happening and may accuse others of "putting these ideas in your head." (This is one reason why a pursuer should not share this book with the distancing partner.) He may become angry, critical, berating, attacking, and spiteful. He may start working late, drinking, ignoring the children, flirting with other women in public, withholding money.

It is important for the pursuer not to be entirely financially dependent on the distancer. If not already working, the pursuer will need to get a job, which has the added advantage of getting the pursuer away from the house. When not at home, the pursuer can be neither baited nor ignored. Instead, she will have the opportunity to meet new people and discover new interests, while also focusing less on the distancer. The most common mistake pursuers make during this time is trying to reason with their irate partners. However, until the last phase of opposition, all such attempts are futile. Like a child's tantrums, the distancer's intense opposition will continue only if the pursuer reacts to it. The pursuer must work hard at not reacting by refraining from trying to "get him to see what he is doing" or reasoning with him or recommending that he "seek help," which will only stimulate further opposition and arguments. The distancer will try to lure the pursuer into these reactive exchanges to wear her down until she gives in, as she has always done before.

If you are a pursuer, concentrate on not defending your actions. Instead, make such "I" statements as "I went out because I wanted to," or "I'm not interested in sex right now," or "I've decided to do something else this weekend," without defending or overly explaining them, as described in the preceding chapters. You may also hear a great deal about how "selfish" you have become, but do not dispute this. So-called selfishness in the pursuit of happiness, dignity, and stability is normal and healthy. During these tense times for both parties, the pursuer's goal is to minimize the reactivity and tension that are bound to occur. The distancer's goal, on the other hand, is to maximize reactivity by confusing the pursuer and provoking reactive turmoil and the resumption of pursuit. This is a time of learning. When (not if) the pursuer finds herself pursuing again, she can learn from the failed attempts. At this point, it can become so unbearable that either the pursuer or the distancer may choose to separate. Regardless of who initiates the separation, the process of pursuit and distance frequently continues even though the parties are living apart. It is up to the pursuer to continue her nonpursuit even when the distancer tries to intimidate her into pursuing and then reconciling on his terms.

### The Distancer's Threatening Phase

In the face of the distancer's threats, the pursuer's primary struggle will be over how strong a stand she takes with him. This will depend on how she feels about the possibility of his leaving her. If she feels she can't cope with a separation (for whatever reason), she will succumb to his threats and go back to pursuing to appease him. This occurs frequently and can simply be approached as another practice shot to be tried again when the pursuer feels stronger.

During this time, the distancer's swings to being pleasant, angry, or threatening will be very rapid. In the words of one pursuing wife, "When I talked to him on the phone yesterday, he said he can't live without me, and today he wants a divorce. It's driving me crazy!" The reason for this behavior is the distancer's inner struggle between wanting to keep to his old ways and fearing that if he does he may actually lose his partner. It comes from the distancer's unavoidable need to work through his own reactions. The pursuer needs to keep this behavior in perspective, neither reacting to it nor losing awareness of her goal.

At this point, both pursuer and distancer are approaching a resolution to their problems. The distancer has tried being agreeable and being angry and threatening, but nothing has worked to restore the familiar pattern of pursuit. The pursuer's unyielding position remains as "I won't be intimidated. I won't go back to the old relationship, no matter how difficult you try to make my life." This leaves the distancer with two options: ending the relationship or making a sincere effort to change. In my professional experience, I have never been able to determine how much caring is left in a relationship before this point. I have seen distancers who reacted relatively mildly and appeared to still care, but, at this point, left their partners. I have also seen distancers who had extremely hostile reactions in which all caring appeared to be gone, but made a choice at this point that showed they still cared a great deal. At this moment, the degree of caring the distancer truly feels will surface in his behavior.

If the distancer has not started or has discontinued his new pursuit within three to four months of the pursuer's detachment, for all practical purposes the relationship is over. If there is no caring left, the pursuer needs to make a decision about whether she will or will not continue in the relationship knowing that this is so. By this time, the pursuer has become much more aware, much stronger, and more autonomous. Some may even have come to the discovery that they want nothing further to do with their partners. One such woman said, "I found out when I stopped my mindless pursuit that it wasn't that I wanted him, but that I was unable to admit I'd failed." However, others may find they still care a great deal. This is a time of decision making for both partners.

## The Point of Realization and Change

Not having been pursued for quite a while, and left alone to confront his own failures, shortcomings, and self-deception, the distancer may move from opposition to honest reevaluation. He will then change if he is going to. If this point is reached and he has not left, it is clear he still cares significantly for his partner. I have found this to be a very reliable observation.

Typically, several things happen at this stage. The distancer, before actually changing, may make a last-ditch effort to bring the relationship back to the previous pattern of pursuit and distance. He may revert to being nice, but with no real change. Indicative of this are glaring inconsistencies between what is said and what is done. For example, one partner reported, "He says he'll stop talking down to me, but he's still doing it." Another said, "She says all the right words but never follows through and changes."

Many distancers become full of self-pity at this point, but it is important that the pursuer not equate this with an effort to change. Self-pity is useless unless a person actually changes, and the distancer must move past this grieving phase toward actually doing something about changing his behavior. The pursuer can now confront the distancer (in a nonreactive way) while he is feeling so empty, confused, and off-balance. It will now be productive to point out his shortcomings because he is as receptive as he will ever be, though the pursuer may feel sorry for the distancer.

Some distancers never move past this stage, choosing to live forever in self-pity, never making the changes that will improve their situation. Instead, they bemoan how hard life has been on them, how their partners never really did "understand" them, how they are innocent and helpless victims at life's mercy. They must move past this point and do so independently. Their partners cannot rescue them or make changes for them. This may be the first and last time the distancer will be truly open to hearing about his shortcomings. Many times distancers talk about getting professional help at this point, and their partners should find out if this is being done. If not, it is an indication of insincerity. For a distancer, counseling at this stage (and only at this stage or beyond) will be beneficial. Feeling lonely, confused, and empty, his defenses are down and he is temporarily open to change. His partner must take the position that the distancer must prove that he has changed by his actions. A husband, for example, may need to prove that he is responsive to his wife and ready to deal with ignored emotional relationship issues, rather than solely providing financial support. During this time, the previous pursuer's feelings will often swing back and forth between wanting him as is, and not wanting anything further to do with him. This is a natural result of her own development and the evolution of the relationship.

When the distancer's actions become consistent with his words, a real change is occurring. However, the pursuer will be wise not to unqualifyingly embrace him or his behavior too soon. It is better for both if she doesn't immediately drop her guard, but continues her nonpursuit and maintains the activities she has developed that do not revolve around, or involve, him.

## When Pursuers and Distancers Experience Change

When a pursuit/distance relationship changes, a variety of different outcomes is possible, depending on the individual partners and the nature of their relationship. The statements below all reflect this variety. They all begin with "I," because they resulted from people learning to live for themselves rather than through or for someone else.

I never thought I would be able to survive living without someone else. I found out I can. I'm a lot stronger than I thought I was. I always believed he was the stronger one. I now realize I may be.

I never did shake free of my pursuit and my dependence on him—even after three years of effort. However, I did keep getting stronger during this time. When my husband finally did have an affair, I was able to handle it. My life was already on its way without him.

After I got out from between him and the children, and stopped accepting responsibility for all the problems in the family, my husband slowly evolved. Eventually he began to do some heavy soul-searching and made some significant changes.

I have gained a realistic view of myself and my life. Before, when I used to live in a make-believe world, I wondered why it was treating me so badly. Now I know.

I decided to separate. At least it's the beginning of something different and the end of something that hadn't been working for a long time.

My life is profoundly different. I no longer get involved with losers who turn out to be distancers. More than that, I finally feel good about myself and the changes I've made in my values and beliefs.

My whole life I had no self-confidence. I was always looking at why I was this way or searching for answers in my past. After stopping my pursuit and successfully confronting myself, I feel such confidence, and I see the beginnings of what I can achieve.

Getting my needs met was all that mattered. When my wife learned she could do without me, my world collapsed. I knew I had to change or lose her, so I changed and feel better as a husband and a person.

When my wife was pursuing me, I knew how to get my way with her. When she stopped, I discovered I couldn't control her any longer. I had to either leave or change. Since I loved her, the only option was to change. I'm so glad I did. We are closer now, and I don't feel smothered by her any more.

When the issue of pursuit and distance is resolved successfully, both individuals and the relationship benefit. But sometimes nothing "works." The pursuer stops pursuing, gets to the end of the process described above, and then finds that somewhere along the way the caring either died or wasn't as deep as believed. The distancer is now treating her better, but she does not love him any longer.

If this is your situation, stopping your pursuit has not been futile. There are still benefits. You will now see your own faults as well as others' realistically; you have developed the knowledge and strength to follow through on changes you were not strong enough to make before. In future relationships, you will not settle for poor treatment or distant partners; you will be able to take corrective action before problems become chronic; if you have children, they will have a better parent and role model; your self-esteem will have increased immeasurably; you will now have the choice and opportunity to pursue satisfying relationships; and, most important, you will no longer be a slave to your cravings and "need" to be loved.

Since I stopped pursuing him and discovered my life went on anyway, I have learned how to enjoy it. Before, I wasn't living, I was existing.

My husband never did change. However, I changed dramatically. I like myself now and feel so happy.

## PURSUIT WORKSHEETS

*You may wish to make several photocopies of the following pages while they are still blank, since you may be repeating these exercises several times.*

If, after reading chapters 8 and 9, you believe you are a pursuer in your relationship, these worksheets are for you. If you are not sure you are a pursuer, or believe you may be one but aren't sure how much you pursue, fill in the worksheets as best you can. They can be of help in clearing up your confusion. If you believe you are a distancer, it is best to give this book to the pursuer in your life, for that will be the most productive way to initiate positive changes in your relationship.

## STOPPING YOUR PURSUIT

As a pursuer, your goal is clearly to stop pursuing. These exercises are designed to help you to accomplish this in several different areas of pursuit. Give examples of how you will stop pursuing in each of the areas below.

1. I will abstain from doing the following:
   Initiating conversation. (For example, "I will not ask her how her day went when she comes home from work.")

_____

_____

   Giving advice unless it's asked for. (For example, "I will stop advising him on how to talk to people.")

_____

_____

   Intervening between him and others. (For example, "I won't send a birthday card to his mother on his behalf.")

_____

_____

   Seeking his advice. (For example, "I will no longer ask him if I'm dressed appropriately for an occasion.")

_____

_____

_____

   Doing the following for him. (For example, "I will stop taking his shirts to the cleaners.")

_____

_____

_____

   Other things I will abstain from doing:

_____

_____

_____

2. I will abstain from doing the following recreational and social activities with my partner. (For example, "I will exercise separately.")

_____

_____

_____

   Other social activities I will abstain from doing:

_____

_____

_____

3. Physically, I will cease initiating:
Hugs and kisses                                                    ☐
Asking my partner if he loves me or how he feels about me    ☐
Having sex with my partner unless I truly desire to          ☐
Other(s):

_____

_____

_____

4. List other areas specific to your situation that you can cease pursuit in.

_____

_____

_____

As you identify new areas in which you pursue, please add them to your worksheets. You may choose to work on all these areas, or you may prefer to concentrate on one—the most common approach—until you are able to stop your pursuit in it, and then add another, and so on. For most people, it is usually best to start with small steps since there will be many inner and external repercussions when you stop pursuing.

5. Do you now feel an urge to share any of this information with your partner?

Please check.

Yes ☐                              No ☐

If you answered yes, describe how you will keep yourself from acting on this impulse. (For example, "I will talk to my neighbor any time I feel I'm about to ask my partner to read this book or share in doing these exercises.")

_____

_____

_____

*Pursuers please note. Pursuers who at this point share this information with their distancer partner immeasurably increase the amount of work and time it takes to resolve their problem.* Do not share this information with your partner. *At least not yet. Continue on with the exercises, and you will find out when it will be helpful to share this material with your partner.*

6. Describe the positive activities you will substitute for the ones you eliminated. (For example, "Instead of talking to my partner, I will talk to my best friend. And to deal with the lack of physical affection, I will hug my sister more often.")

_____

_____

_____

7. As discussed earlier, rarely do pursuers stop doing all of these actions at once. Rather, most do it piecemeal. Describe your plan for enacting the above changes. (For example, "I will begin by no longer picking up and then washing clothes he leaves on the floor.")

_____

_____

_____

8. Describe the external repercussions of the actions listed above and your inner reactions. (For example, "If I don't do his laundry, he will let his dirty clothes pile up and I won't be able to stand it.")

_____

_____

_____

## DEALING WITH THE LACK OF CARING

As you begin to stop your pursuit, the issue of whether or not your partner cares for you will surface. The following exercises will help you deal with your wish for the caring that your partner does not provide. (This need for caring has been the fuel for your pursuit.)

1. Describe what it feels like when you think you will never do anything together with your partner again. (For example, "When I think of this, I feel very hurt.")

_____

_____

_____

2. Describe what it feels like when you think your partner will never be the warm and involved companion you had hoped for. (For example, "I feel like I've been betrayed.")

_____

_____

_____

3. Describe what it feels like when you think your partner will never:
   Change. (For example, "I feel hopeless.")

   _____

   _____

   _____

   Appreciate you. (For example, "I feel like a fool.")

   _____

   _____

   _____

   Need you. (For example, "I feel so useless.")

   _____

   _____

   _____

4. Describe what it feels like when you think your partner:
   Doesn't care about you. (For example, "I feel very angry.")

   _____

   _____

   _____

   Never did care about you. (For example, "I feel used.")

   _____

   _____

   _____

   Will never care about you. (For example, "I feel so empty and lonely.")

   _____

   _____

   _____

The above exercises can be very painful. Their purpose is to remove the fuel for your pursuit. The need to be cared about in order to feel good about yourself causes uncontrollable pursuit. Until this need for caring is dealt with, controlling your pursuit is going to be difficult. These exercises are not meant to be filled in at one sitting. Keep coming back to them to fill in missing pieces or to expand on what is there. When you no longer feel overly upset as you do these exercises, you have sufficiently resolved them to move on.

5. List who you can talk to about these feelings. (For example, "My friend Sue at work." "My pastor at church.")

_____

_____

_____

## DEALING WITH THE LACK OF PROGRESS

1. Very likely your partner will want know why you are making these changes in your behavior. Anticipating his queries, write your reason here. Make it a clear and short "I" statement with as few specific details as possible. At this stage, it is best to keep your intentions to yourself. (For example, "I feel some changes are called for on my part.")

_____

_____

_____

It is extremely rare for a pursuer to be able to stop pursuing completely and immediately. Instead, most pursuers initially waver between pursuing and not pursuing. The following exercises will help you deal with this problem.

2. If you find yourself unable to consistently stop your pursuit, check which of the reasons below cause your hesitation.

I want a guarantee that this will work before I start.                    ☐

I want approval of my efforts before I begin.                              ☐

I want my partner to reciprocate or take the lead in making
   changes before I start.                                                ☐

I am fearful my partner will leave me.                                     ☐

I fear I will have a difficult time following through after my
   initial efforts.                                                       ☐

Other reasons:

_____

_____

_____

3. Expand on your reasons here. (For example, "I decided to stop my pursuit, tried it for a few days, then became fearful I'd end up being all alone, and I began pursuing again. I hate my cowardice.")

_____

_____

_____

   Part or all of the above exercises are likely to be causing you a good deal of anxiety and upset. Such feelings are normal for pursuers when they first stop pursuing. It is essential that you learn how to cope with this discomfort. The following set of exercises will help you in this task.

4. Check off which of the following you feel when you stop your pursuit. I feel:

| | | | |
|---|---|---|---|
| Cheated | ☐ | Selfish | ☐ |
| Confused | ☐ | Hurt | ☐ |
| Afraid | ☐ | Angry | ☐ |
| Self-doubtful | ☐ | That I've failed | ☐ |
| As if I died inside | ☐ | | |

   Explain when you feel the above. (For example, "When I don't ask my partner if he still loves me, I feel as if I died inside.")

_____

_____

_____

   When you stop your pursuit, you will be struggling with difficult feelings. For most pursuers these feelings will be intense and profound and must not be disregarded. You can get help by talking to a therapist or a trusted friend about these feelings.

## DEALING WITH YOUR INNER RESISTANCE

1. All pursuers experience an inner struggle between wanting to stop their pursuit and wanting to continue it. Describe your own struggle here. (For example, "Part of me says I shouldn't go through all of this, and another part says I don't have any choice.")

_____

_____

_____

2. Very likely you will experience sudden and intense mood swings during this internal struggle. Describe them here. (For example, "One day I feel so much relief and feel good. The next day I feel so empty and down I can't get out of bed without a great deal of effort.")

_____

_____

_____

3. Put any anger you feel toward your partner to constructive use. Rather than staying angry at your partner for what "he did," describe here what you can do differently to prevent being caught up in your anger in the future. (For example, "Rather than getting angry at my boyfriend for standing me up so many times, I need to redirect my anger at my own habit of keeping such low standards that I put up with such treatment.")

_____

_____

_____

Following is a list of Do's and Don'ts that you may want to refer to occasionally.

| Do | Don't |
| --- | --- |
| Refrain from pursuit. | Get preoccupied with wanting |
| Rechannel your pain toward | to know why your partner |
| overcoming your own | and you behave as you do. |
| shortcomings. | Do anything spiteful. |

| | |
|---|---|
| Seek professional help if you feel suicidal or continually depressed. | Blame your partner. |
| | Do anything impulsive. |
| Be very selective about accepting advice from others. | Provoke arguments. |
| | Become reactive. |
| Learn patience. | |

4. Feelings of loneliness and the fear of being alone and "without someone" can become very intense for many pursuers after they stop their pursuit. If you have this fear, describe it here. (For example, "I'm afraid I no longer have any purpose in life.")

_____

_____

_____

5. Describe how you will deal with this fear. (For example, "I will begin talking about it to a counselor or a close friend.")

_____

_____

_____

   Note: If these feelings become overwhelming, allow yourself to start pursuing again and seek out the help of a professional counselor or psychotherapist. With this help you can again attempt to stop pursuit. The fear of being alone is a very common and normal one. For most people, resolving it is a long-term struggle. The purpose of the above two exercises is to help you identify it as an issue that you need to address.

## DEALING WITH YOUR SHORTCOMINGS

The following exercises are designed to help you identify and overcome your shortcomings.

1. Since the low feelings you are experiencing provide good motivation for confronting them, check off the following common weaknesses of pursuers that you recognize as your own.

| | | | |
|---|---|---|---|
| I am defensive | ☐ | I am overly dependent | |
| I am overly responsible | ☐ | on others | ☐ |

I have unbending expec-
  tations of others          ☐

I am emotionally
  reactive                   ☐

I appease others             ☐

I am overinvolved
  with the children          ☐

I tend to blame others          ☐

I control/manipulate others  ☐

I am impatient                  ☐

I am overly nice and
  trusting                      ☐

I am an approval-seeker         ☐

I am unable to follow
  through on changing           ☐

Other(s)

_____

_____

2. Further describe your shortcomings. (For example, "I have a hard time trying not to control the actions of others around me and reducing my expectations of family members. I find it hard to stop allowing myself to be used as a 'doormat' by others.")

_____

_____

_____

3. Describe how you will begin to decrease or eliminate the above short-comings. (For example, "I will watch myself closely to restrain myself from being too defensive. I will begin to limit my critical comments to others.")

_____

_____

_____

## DEALING WITH YOUR PARTNER'S OPPOSITION

While you are dealing with the above issues, you'll have opposition by your partner. The following set of exercises is geared to help you antici-pate your partner's opposition. Use a pencil to fill in how you believe he will act, and then go back and correct it in ink if his actual response is dif-ferent. Remember, with some distancers, the ugliness stage precedes the niceness stage. If this is true in your situation, simply fill in that exercise first.

## Coping With the "Nice" Stage

1. Niceness: Describe how your partner will be "nice" to you. (For example, "I expect he will clean up after himself and turn on the charm.")

_____

_____

_____

2. List the fears and concerns you have when he acts so "nice" and you don't start pursuing again. (For example, "I feel like I'll push him away permanently.")

_____

_____

_____

3. Few pursuers don't succumb to their distancer's new "niceness" (adopted in response to the new absence of pursuit). Describe what happened between you when you started pursuing again. (For example, "He was so nice to me that I felt very guilty for not doing certain things for him any more. So I started doing those things again. Shortly afterward, he went back to his old selfish and uncaring self.")

_____

_____

_____

4. Describe here what you will do differently the next time he becomes "nice" in response to your nonpursuit. (For example, "I will restrain myself from doing things for him again.")

_____

_____

_____

5. Does he make promises he doesn't carry out?
Yes ☐                                No ☐

   If you answered yes, list those broken promises here. (For example, "He promised he would start spending more time with the children and me.")

_____

_____

_____

6. Describe how you will use the anger you feel toward your partner about breaking his promises to make positive changes in yourself. (For example, "Instead of getting angry at him when he calls to ask me out to dinner, I will be angry for having been too trusting in the past. When he calls, I won't at first accept his invitation.)

_____

_____

_____

   Note: Please keep in mind that failures are almost universal at this point. So don't get disheartened; simply use them to learn from your mistakes.

### Coping With the "Ugly" Stage

1. Describe how your partner blames you. (For example, "He says it's my fault we are getting along so poorly and that I'm too selfish. In fact, he's the one who always has to get his way.")

_____

_____

_____

2. Check off how you think your partner will try to pressure you into returning to your old behavior and pursuing again.
He will:

Try to make me feel guilty ☐        Act spiteful and provocative   ☐
Accuse and blame me        ☐        Berate and criticize me        ☐
Get angry at me             ☐        Other(s)

_____

_____

_____

3. Describe in detail how he will pressure you. (For example, "My partner will attack my friends, tell me I'm trying to break up our family, cut me off from all financial sources.")

_____

_____

_____

Most people respond to such pressures by trying to reason with their partners. The following exercises will help you see the futility of trying to get "through" to your partner during this stage.

4. List the dates you have and have not been able to "reason" with your partner.
Dates I have succeeded in reasoning with my partner:

_____

_____

_____

Dates I have not succeeded in reasoning with my partner:

_____

_____

_____

5. List the dates you've urged your partner to "seek counseling" and the dates he has done so.
Dates I have urged my partner to seek help:

_____

_____

_____

Dates my partner sought help:

_____

_____

_____

6. If your partner sought counseling, check whether it has helped or not.
Yes  ☐                              No  ☐

If you answered yes, consider yourself one of the fortunate few. If you answered no, don't worry about it. Either way, simply continue with the exercises.

7. Which of the following accusations does your partner make?

That you are seeing another man/woman ☐

That you do not love your partner any longer ☐

All of the problems are your meddlesome friends' fault ☐

You are being a poor parent ☐

You are being selfish ☐

Other(s)

_____

_____

_____

8. Describe these accusations in detail. (For example, "He says I'm so selfish, but all I want is for him to show some caring for me.")

_____

_____

_____

Following is a list of Do's and Don'ts that may be helpful to refer back to occasionally.

| Do | Don't |
|---|---|
| Make yourself financially independent (if possible). | Try to reason with your partner. |
| Make simple "I" statements. | Try to get your partner to seek help. |
| Look for consistency between your partner's actions. | Defend or explain your own words and actions. |
| Try to "get through" to your partner. | Vent either negative or positive feelings to your partner. |
| Mentally rehearse your words and actions in advance. | |
| Vent your feelings to a trusted friend. | |
| Try to anticipate your partner's actions. | |
| Study and learn from your unsuccessful efforts. | |

Please refer back to chapters 3, 5, and especially 6 to refresh your memory about how to handle your partner's attacks, which will be particularly intense during this period.

9. Below, fill in the dates of your unsuccessful attempts to keep from defending yourself against your partner's attacks.

| | | | |
|---|---|---|---|
| 1st missed opportunity | ☐ | 6th missed opportunity | ☐ |
| 2nd missed opportunity | ☐ | 7th missed opportunity | ☐ |
| 3rd missed opportunity | ☐ | 8th missed opportunity | ☐ |
| 4th missed opportunity | ☐ | 9th missed opportunity | ☐ |
| 5th missed opportunity | ☐ | 10th missed opportunity | ☐ |

10. The caring you feel toward your partner will go through changes. One minute/day/week you will feel one way; the next minute/day/week you will feel different. Describe that wavering here. (For example, "One week I don't know what I'll do without him. The next week I wish he'd leave, I hate him so much.")

_____

_____

_____

This is the longest and most difficult phase of your work, so please don't give up. Instead, learn from your failures what you can change to make the next encounter with your partner more successful.

## DEALING WITH YOUR PARTNER'S THREATS

1. List the threats your partner will make. (For example, "He'll tell me it's over and it'll be my fault.")

_____

_____

_____

2. As discussed earlier, your partner's swings between treating you nicely and wanting to reconcile, and treating you harshly with no desire to reconcile are very common. Those mood swings can be very disconcerting. However, they are indicative of his internal struggle over whether or not

to change. Describe your partner's mood swings. (For example, "One minute he says he loves me and can't live without me, the next he's telling me he hates me and wants me to leave.")

_____

_____

_____

3. Name someone you can talk to, who will support you through this difficult period. (For example, "I will talk to my sister, who is always level-headed about things like this.")

_____

_____

_____

## WORKING THROUGH TO THE STAGE OF POSITIVE CHANGE

1. Describe the areas where your partner's actions are inconsistent with his words. (For example, "He says he loves me and wants to be together, yet he is still living with his girlfriend.")

_____

_____

_____

2. Describe the changes you want to see in your partner. (For example, "No more angry outbursts, no more jealousy.")

_____

_____

_____

3. The following checklist will help you determine if your partner is now sincere about making changes. If even just one of these items is not checked off, I would question your partner's motives.

He is:

| | |
|---|---|
| Acknowledging his faults | ☐ |
| Following through on the changes he says he is going to make | ☐ |
| Putting you before himself | ☐ |
| Voluntarily attending counseling (which is productive at this stage, but not before) | ☐ |

4. If you believe his changes to be sincere, describe the pursuit areas you will initially avoid resuming. (For example, "I will not clean up after him, have sex when I don't want to, go only to the movies he wants to see, give up my friends or activities, or wrap my life around his.")

_____

_____

_____

5. Describe how you will delay resuming complete involvement with your partner. Include time limits. (For example, "Before three months are up, I will not go to any movies I don't want to see. For that time, I will also maintain a separate checking account.")

_____

_____

_____

6. Describe how and when you will resume your complete involvement with your partner. (For example, "By six months I will begin to go to movies he wants to see, but I will still insist that he go to movies that interest me. I will also open a shared checking account, while still maintaining my own account.")

_____

_____

_____

7. If your partner has made sincere changes and wants to reconcile, you can now share chapters 8 and 9 (including these worksheets) with your partner.

8. Describe how you will maintain your nonpursuit. (For example, "After one year, I will still keep my own friends and have my own checking account, nor will I start to cater to him again.")

_____

_____

_____

9. Describe how you will always behave in relation to your partner. (For example, "I plan never to allow myself to be talked down to, followed around with anger, or pushed into giving up my friends.")

_____

_____

_____

10. Sometimes the changes that distancers (as well as pursuers) make don't last and they go back to their old behaviors (no guarantees). List any signs that indicate your partner may be going back to his prior distancing ways. (For example, "He is starting to drink, beginning to get mad when I don't do things his way. He is acting jealous without cause.")

_____

_____

_____

11. List any signs that will indicate to you that you are starting to pursue again. (For example, "If I begin to feel responsible for everything again and seem exhausted all the time.")

_____

_____

_____

If, in the future, you begin pursuing again or your partner starts distancing in a regular pattern, go back to the beginning of chapter 9 and redo the steps that will again free you.

Congratulations! Stopping pursuit *and* dealing with the repercussions is a tremendous feat. Give yourself the recognition you deserve for this effort.

CONCLUSION

# Separation and Reconciliation

In trying to resolve relationship conflict, many people end up separating for a variety of reasons. Not infrequently, the initial increase in tension created by changes being made is too much for the already over-strained relationship to handle. Despite all efforts to stop pursuit, control reactivity and carry on with your life, it becomes impossible to continue living together and the decision to separate is made. Sometimes, one or both parties find their love is gone and often with it their purpose in staying together. Frequently, distancers want out of the relationship sometime during the described process, only to find they care more for their partner than they previously thought. Separation does not mean divorce is inevitable. On the contrary, it leads to the conditions necessary for positive change to occur, which lead to reconciliation.

The process of separation and reconciliation is profoundly painful and confusing. Both parties are filled with tremendous emotional cross-currents—whether this is the right thing to do; whether they should stay separated or whether they should reconcile; whether they still care enough for their partner to attempt reconciliation; whether their partner has actually changed, and if so, will it last? The questions you can ask yourself are almost limitless.

Because of the emotional upset, separation is frequently a time of ambiguity for both parties: *One day I want him back, the next day I don't. Then he wants me back, then he doesn't.* There are tremendous mood swings: *One minute I feel good, the next I feel horrible.* And confusion: *I don't know whether or not to end it. I don't know where to go from here.*

Why the ambiguity and mood swings? Separation is a profound change in someone's life. As with all change, part of you wants it and part of you resists it. The bigger the change, the bigger the internal tug-of-war. In spite of this emotional tangle, a break-up can have a positive effect on a couple's reconciliation. Many couples need to go through the emotional low that separation causes before they can sort out their issues together.

Use the pain and turmoil of separation to reflect, identify and confront your own faults. The point of this book has been to show that responding with reactive behavior (even in your own defense) is as faulty as your partner's initial antagonism. Likewise, pursuers are as responsible as distancers for the problems in the relationship, and for the solution (or lack thereof). Push yourself to get past the pain you feel. Stop blaming your partner. Use the previous chapters to help you identify changes that need to be made.

## A Word to Distancers

If you find yourself hurting, open to change and wanting your partner back (who is now quite unapproachable if not outright hostile), the situation is not necessarily as hopeless as it may appear. Keep in mind that although it "takes two" to reconcile, it only takes one to start the reconciliation process.

In response to hurt, indifference and distance in the relationship, your pursuer has slowly erected an emotional wall around herself—coldness, hostility, resentment. Your goal will be to dismantle this wall. In order to do so you must understand how it developed. At the root is her belief that you don't care for her and haven't for a long time. This comes from experiencing years of your lack of approval, warmth and involvement. Remember, pursuers are feeling-oriented people, not object-oriented people. Working two jobs to provide her with objects and possessions is not necessarily interpreted as caring by the pursuer even if she enjoyed the material benefits. Instead, she saw your distance (absence due to work) as self-centeredness, and perhaps attempted dominance as proof of your lack of love. By showing her you have changed through behavior and not by words alone, you have a much better chance of being believed.

Patience, patience and more patience is required. During this period, loneliness is usually so great that you will become extremely impatient and desire reconciliation immediately. However, her wall has been building over a long period. It will take time (frequently many months, maybe a year or more) to break it down. She may not believe that you are sincere in your efforts if you have made many previous promises that have not been followed through.

I have seen couples I had no doubt would reconcile, yet they did not. Likewise, I have seen some of the most horrendous separations which I believed could never work out, and yet did. In my experience the only way to proceed is to continue in spite of your partner's coldness, assuming it is the correct path until all behavior indicates otherwise. Since she is going through an internal struggle between reconciling and not reconciling, you may begin to see some of this in her behavior. She may be "nice" one day, then cold and verbally abusive the next. When the niceness occurs, it is important that you not get your expectations and hopes up. Do not put pressure on her to return; do not drop your changes. This is the most common error I have seen and accounts for 90% of all failures where success could have been possible. Especially avoid all threats and attempts at intimidation. In short, you will have to implement the changes you are making, despite the lack of any positive feedback.

Concentrate on showing how *your* behavior has permanently changed. Most, if not all, pursuers have been repeatedly faced with spouses who have promised to make the necessary changes, only to have those changes dropped as soon as the relationship is healing. The pursuer may well, and rightfully, demand an extended period of clear-cut change before she is willing to consider reconciliation.

Over the course of time, the pursuer has become acutely sensitive to tone of voice, subtle put-downs, indirect blame, and even slight indications of selfishness. Even a simple phone conversation will indicate whether you are still behaving in a selfish and counter-productive manner. It can also indicate whether you are accepting responsibility and developing a more caring attitude.

Keep in mind that the pursuer has spent years ignoring her own wants and needs in an attempt to please you, assure your happiness and gain your approval. Pursuers are very dedicated and determined people. For a long time, she has been dedicated to your comfort. It has taken years of being downtrodden for her to decide that if she does not attend to her own needs, then no one else is going to do so. It is unrealistic to expect her to jump (again) because you promise that this time things will be different.

Focus on winning her back through love, humility and selfless-ness. Involve yourself in her life. Return the respect, caring and un-derstanding that you have received from her. This is much more likely to be successful than threats, blame, control, or domination.

*The Solo Partner* explains the valuable opportunities within a mar-riage for self-change. Necessity for change, however, does not end at the point of separation. The need for change continues—as do the costs and consequences of not changing. Indeed, separation pro-vides almost ideal conditions for change to occur. People frequently report that their relationship is better after the reconciliation than it had been for many years prior to separating. In fact, it is precisely be-cause of the disappointment and hurt that separation can have ben-eficial effects. At your lowest point, the motivation for constructive change is at its peak and the opportunity for self and relationship growth is tremendous. Though it is a difficult and painful time, the potential for long-term, beneficial growth is enormous. In the ab-sence of someone to blame for your problems, you have the time and space to look honestly at yourself and evaluate your part in those problems. This can lead to reconciliation with a powerful dif-ference—a relationship built on a firm and positive new base.